A TWENTIETH-CENTURY ARGONAUT

ONE MAN'S QUEST FOR AN AMERICAN DREAM

ERNEST BALDINI

iUniverse LLC
Bloomington

A TWENTIETH-CENTURY ARGONAUT
ONE MAN'S QUEST FOR AN AMERICAN DREAM

iUniverse books may be ordered through booksellers or by contacting:

iUniverse LLC
1663 Liberty Drive
Bloomington, IN 47403
www.iuniverse.com
1-800-Authors (1-800-288-4677)

ISBN: 978-1-4917-1126-2 (sc)
ISBN: 978-1-4917-1128-6 (hc)
ISBN: 978-1-4917-1127-9 (e)

Library of Congress Control Number: 2013918769

Printed in the United States of America.

iUniverse rev. date: 10/21/2013

"To reach your dream, sometimes you first
have to go through a nightmare"

–Ernest Baldini, 2013

TABLE OF CONTENTS

DEDICATION

To Jean, my love, for all the years of friendship and adventure

To my father, who said, "Never believe your own propaganda"

To my mother, who readied me for the worst, and the best

To Anita, and Rick, for showing us how to cope with life's challenges through love, and perseverance

To Marc, for fulfilling his grandfather's dream by becoming still another pioneer in flight

To Pam, for her caring and support through it all

FOREWORD

If you think about it, we don't know a lot about our friends unless they choose to tell us. For earlier generations friends were usually neighbors. Today, friendships often develop through associations. So a man may greet his neighbor in the morning as he backs his car out of the driveway, but he has a much closer relationship with a committee member of his Florida Bar chapter, a fellow deacon in his church, and the sailor whose boat is in a slip next to his at the local marina.

While this may be true, it is also true that meetings centered around these associations are often driven by an agenda, formal or informal. So when you visit your boat, you find yourself talking to this "neighbor" about the new commodore, the weather, or the gulls that are messing up your canvas. With our busy lives it's hard to get to know each other.

I felt I knew Ernie Baldini well for the past few decades. We have counted each other good friends. We met at Florida Trail Association events and found camaraderie in building the organization. I also know Jean well. I knew they had kids. Knew he was an engineer. Knew he worked "at the Cape." That sort of thing.

But then I read his book . . . and found out how much I didn't know . . . including lots of exciting stuff at the Cape. When Ernie said good morning to "Werner," it wasn't Werner Jones or Werner Smith; it was Werner von Braun! When an Atlas-Centaur launch was aborted at T-minus-zero seconds, it was Ernie's finger on the cut-off button.

By the way, an apropos line from Ernie's book: "At this very moment, the Voyager spacecraft, powered into Earth escape trajectory by a Centaur in 1977, is just now leaving the solar system and entering inter-stellar space."

As fascinating as the Argonaut stories are, Ernie's life has been so rich that the other chapters pull you in, too, from climbing Mt. Rainier to diving off St. Johns in the Caribbean. I knew Ernie served on the board of the Florida Trail Association and was its treasurer and president, and I knew he served on the board of the American Hiking Society; I helped lure him into that job, but then I found out just how active Ernie was in many other things by reading his book.

Not long ago Ernie pulled into my driveway with an odd assortment of radio antennas sticking out of the roof of his van like some huge pin cushion. Which reminded me just how experienced he was as a ham radio operator. And does he have stories to tell about that!

Every chapter of this Argonaut's life has been enriched by the ideal wife he found to share it with. He never lets you forget how fortunate he feels about this.

If you are Ernie's next-door neighbor and have hung on the fence, beer in hand, and shot the breeze over those decades on Cocoa Beach, you probably know all of this. For all the others, an armchair travel of galactic dimension awaits you.

Jim Kern

Author, *Trail Reflections, 50 Years of Hiking & Backpacking*
Author, *The Wildlife Art & Adventures of Jim Kern Photographer*
Founder, Florida Trail Association
Co-Founder, American Hiking Society
Founder, Big City Mountaineers

PREFACE

As my life evolved and experiences mounted, I became known among family and friends for telling tales of my life, career, travel, and encounters with famous people. Even though these events were not heroic, fantastic or worldwide, these same family and friends urged me to write a book. After my retirement, I was asked to tell my life story to a local club. I considered it an honor and diligently set about the task.

I thought the presentation took too much time but my audience did not respond that way. Their attention was riveted to my next words throughout the event. At the finish, they stood up with sustained applause.

That day I realized something significant. I had lived an American dream. It was what I was enabled to accomplish in a free society, given humble beginnings and a free education. In review my realized dream was complete with love, family, faith, adventure, financial security, and self-confidence, without the diversions of greed, lust, envy or addiction. I had lived while examining the consequences of my striving, and found balance. The closure of my life span has therefore been peaceful and reflective.

So this record is written herein to provide an example of one American life, its choices and outcomes.

I hope my readers will find some parallels with their lives, and realize their fulfillment, or that, if in youth, they plan well their American dream still to be realized.

INTRODUCTION

This book is about me, a cross-eyed kid from Detroit's east side, who, born into the Great Depression, reached adulthood in post-World War II and became a rocket scientist. In doing so, I experienced my version of an American dream. My story is not about money, or houses, or cars, but about doing the best one can, taking pride in workmanship, making contributions to society and serving your country. The love of parents and family, the dedication of teachers, the cruelness of bullying, and the rigors of the military were all factors that shaped my life. Varied happenings brought me excitement and happiness and gave me endurance and courage, and caused me to realize no one achieves their dream alone. Thus prepared, the end years of my life are tranquil and contributory. This is the story of that life that spans eighty-seven years, at this writing.

The title of this book, and strangely its theme, honors the name of my high school homeroom. The crew of the mythical Greek ship, the Argo, with Jason as their leader, sailed the sea in search of the Golden Fleece.

I take the reader through some of the events in the science and turbulence of the twentieth century, illustrating ideas and incidents in my life that created career and character-shaping opportunities. Some ideas are time-proven examples that handicap strengthens character. Others are as simple as developing a sense of history. My life was not unique. It has parallels in the lives of millions of Americans whose years have been clouded by wars, disasters, and financial cycles, but who have gone on to live proud lives with loving families and friends.

As my biography unfolds into an era of postwar prosperity, and my dream is realized, I share experiences in emerging technologies. I note my meetings with historical figures such as Edward Teller and Wernher Von Braun. I relate my participation in technological history, and I weave the ambiance of travel, romance and recreation into my story. I insert into this life thread my religious faith, not to proselytize but to illustrate that every life needs a binding philosophy. I describe the awfulness of Hurricane Andrew. I mix hubris with fear. I write about living through an inspiring and truly mountain-top experience. I serve and thereby realize the satisfaction of volunteerism. I travel unusual roads learning about my countrymen, and I close with advisory words about the finality that everyone faces.

CHAPTER 1

TO BE BULLIED OR BETTER?

It was 1934 and I was eight years old and taking my first elevator ride. My mother, father and I were in the Penobscot Building in Detroit headed for the upper-floor offices of an ophthalmologist. The reason: to have my crossed eye "straightened" in an in-office procedure. The starts and stops of our ascent were slightly nauseating me, and I clutched my parents' hands tightly as I pondered the impending operation. We arrived at our floor and walked into the dark wood-paneled offices of the eye doctor. As they led me to the operating table, the window view from the height of the skyscraper added to my nausea. I was scared and trembling as they collectively prepared me for the surgery.

The concept of this procedure was to correct this strabismus by pulling the side muscle of the crossed eye into straightness. This action was to be performed concurrent with my observations of an eye chart. I look back on that 1934 medical science as the best available for the time and a loving action by my parents, who had spent hard-earned money in the middle of the Great Depression. The procedure was not a complete success and for the rest of my life I never told my mother and father of the failings.

In the weeks that followed, my eye healed and I was fitted for glasses. The frames were of steel and the lenses were thick but I could see and read very well. To an eight year old, that was OK. But soon, I began to experience the down side. "Hey, four eyes, catch the ball, dummy!" was the taunt as other kids would test my young athleticism by throwing a very fast baseball at me. The same was true when I was at bat. Still deeper were the feelings when there was a scrub game forming and players were being chosen. As one would expect, I was always one of the last to be chosen by reluctant captains.

I did not realize at the time that building inside my brain was the idea that I would find some way to show these bullies what I could do well. I did turn to my parents, and to my close friends, for some counsel on these matters, and their help bonded me to them for life. Dad pitched many a ball to me, Mom counseled me after incidents of rejection, and my close childhood friends shared their similar experiences with me.

One of the ways I found to cope with this social sadness was, obviously, to study hard and get good grades. Still, my effort had its downside when I was called the hackneyed term "teachers pet". I learned quickly that the taunters were covering their failures. Good grades made teachers notice me, and so in the remaining years in grade school I was often picked to lead whatever class program was happening. I was usually reluctant and not happy with the extra work of leading but I accepted it, knowing my parents would not approve of me being shy and reticent. It was the beginning of a trait of accepting leadership, reluctantly, and then performing well.

Since baseball was a sport that always reminded me of the taunts, I usually just watched the games. Meanwhile I found basketball when I got my first summer job at a YMCA. My task was to keep the gym equipment in order and repair. I began to shoot baskets whenever I had time. I realized that "four-eyes" was making swish shots from the corner. One of my teacher-counselors in Hi-Y coached me along in dribbling and passing. While I never made the junior or senior high school varsities, I slowly shed, among my peers, the taunts and bullying, and was often picked early for scrub basketball teams. I always watched for other "four-eyed" kids and helped build their self-esteem.

At this period in my young teen life I was undergoing another learning experience of which I was unaware. Saturday afternoon movies that I frequently attended were a set of morality plays about the bad guys, the heroes, the rescuing forces coming over the hill, and the protection of the damsel in distress.

Great Depression kids were used to receiving only one present for Christmas, and one year mine was a chemistry set. I became enthralled with science and Buck Rogers in space. I experimented with chemicals that were dangerous and burned holes in our back yard concrete driveway. Fascinated with such power, I began to draw rocket ships, read every space ship comic book that I could find, and yearned to get to high school and take science classes. Yet I had no idea I would someday be a rocket scientist.

I was fortunate that my father, who had become an auto production line wizard, kept his job through the depressed years. He was a great engineer, without a degree, who learned through correspondence schools. He tutored me well in many fundamentals of good design, cost control, quality assurance, and, most of important of all, critical thinking.

We young ones in the neighborhood did not, at the time, know the dreaded Mafia was so close, next door. My mother and father, proud law-abiding Italian-American parents, did not allow us to mix with the children from that house. I recall the big, black sedans and touring cars in which the bosses would come and go. Later in my army days, while wielding a submachine gun, I realized why they always wore large, long overcoats.

As I grew, my mother's family of sisters and their families had migrated together in Detroit. We would have Sunday dinners together with discussions about politics, war, religion, and people. I learned much from my elders at those events. The stereotype of an Italian family had emerged in our society and I realized how ours was in juxtaposition to those other Italian-Americans. Our family's men were honest, dedicated men: a lawyer, an accountant, a civil engineer, and my Dad. I remembered all my life my father saying, "Son, it will take a lot of Baldinis to counter what those bastards (the Mafia) have done."

CHAPTER 2

WAR CLOUDS

It was a gloomy and overcast day, and our bunker was damp with humidity and sweat. I was assigned sniper duty at the rim trench, to watch for the enemy to raise their heads. Then, terrified, I saw and centered one of them in my gunsight, and pulled the trigger . . . . POW! . . . . the rubber gun shot its energy at my neighbor buddy, just as my mother called me for lunch from the vacant lot that separated our house from the one next door. My friends and I were beginning to emulate the armies battling with the Nazis in faraway Europe. Soldiers yes, but we were careful to not imitate gangsters.

That summer while in New York with my parents, I witnessed the reality of the Nazi logo. I was with some cousins and hearing a loud, steady drone, everyone began to look up, pointing at a giant dirigible slowly crossing the area. It was the transoceanic German zeppelin *Hindenburg* heading toward the U. S. Navy airbase at Lakehurst, New Jersey. It was startling to see an actual Nazi swastika on a giant German airship. I was not old enough to realize the airship used hydrogen for lift, or to have any idea that someday I, and my son, would be in the forefront of flight using that same element in rockets, and that I would know, in the first person, the immigrant Germans who would lead the launch of a giant rocket to the moon.

I remember the anguish and horror of the radio broadcast when, on one of its next visits, May 6, 1937, the Hindenburg exploded at Lakehurst as it moored. I thought of the dangers my father experienced when, as a young mechanic in 1919, he served on the ground crew at Roosevelt Field, New York, for the mooring of the hydrogen-filled British dirigible R-34.

As time passed, leadership opportunities in school coupled with discipline by my parents, and bolstered by films from Hollywood, were continuing to contribute to the formation of my character. The movie industry was slowly motivating America toward action in the war in Europe. Every film had a message, honor and integrity were highlights, and fairness and democracy were evident in every portrayal of a citizen meeting. Filthy four letter words did not yet emanate from Hollywood.

My parents took me to the 1939 New York World's Fair. The theme structure was the Trylon and Perisphere. The Trylon resembled the present day TransAmerica building in San Francisco and the Perisphere had a Walt Disney World Epcot earth look. What so impressed me was that inside the Perisphere was a world of the future in miniature. Visitors were presented with a panoramic view of an American landscape, complete with superhighways, and modernistic buildings. Every time I look down on present day America while in flight, I see that same fair view. Perhaps President Eisenhower did also, and later, so ordered the Interstate Highway System into being. It was a vision of my dream America that was still to come but also a harbinger of an automotive stampede that would dissect cities and towns.

My paternal grandfather was with us that day. He had participated in some of the startling beginnings of the twentieth century, amongst them, flight. As a cabinetmaker apprentice, in Italy, he had helped produce wooden propellers for Louis Bleriot's planes, one of which was the first to fly the English Channel. The specter of war hung over that World's Fair, especially the German and Italian participation. When we went into the Italian building, there stood a larger-than-life statute of Mussolini. My grandfather, a lifelong student of Italian republican politics, raised his cane in anger at the figure, and was frowned upon by two Fascist black-shirted guards. We had to pull him away as he hurled curses at the black marble statute. The passion he had for his politics impressed me that day and I took on some of his character. In visits to see him later in my life, I learned, through his broken English, of his pride in his work, and his sense of ethics.

One other event involving the fair, that I recalled with amazement years later, was visiting the AT&T exhibit. A voice encoder with a keyboard was demonstrated by a young woman. She asked my name and then I heard it called out in low, baritone mechanical speech from the machine. This invention was the forerunner of a secret cryptographic device that would greatly aid the winning of World War II.

At my grade school, which was built to resemble Independence Hall in Philadelphia, my history teacher, Mr. Freeman, a kind Jewish man, was periodically bringing us stories about his relatives escaping from persecution in Germany. His tales kept us aware of the menace building in Europe, and our young minds wondered why America didn't react to that.

As the coming war rumbled in the distance across the sea, the echoes of the previous one were still evident in our neighborhood. One of my girl friends, a Heidi-like Teutonic beauty of German parents, went home each day to a father who was a veteran of the Kaiser's German army. I didn't realize at the time that this German immigrant, and my father, were part of the automobile industry that grew and the war effort that emerged as part of a great migration from Europe. It was composed of machinists and tool-and-die makers. They came from Bohemia, Bavaria, Slovakia, Austria, and Germany. While their agricultural brethren settled the great plains, they settled Detroit, Dayton, Toledo, and the other industrial cities.

In the growing conflicts of 1939 and on, Dad was busy with engineering development of the B-17 Flying Fortress bomber belly turret, and with other weapons manufacturing, supplying the allied nations efforts in Europe in the war against the Nazis. Mom was dutifully collecting scrap aluminum, cans, and other commodities important to a war effort, and cooking meals with rationed foods. I knew America would be in a war over there within a year or two. As youths in junior and senior high school, the war loomed large in our lives and throttled the usual teen–age carefree life style. The boys of my generation began to focus on what they would do in the military.

Living near the Canadian border, we were aware that the U. S. Coast Guard had been busy chasing smugglers during the Prohibition era but by 1939 it was organizing for war. It had to form an auxiliary to help with its duties. Dad had a friend who owned a thirty-foot boat moored at one of the Detroit River marinas, and he would often take me to it. I remembered that his friend was a member of the Coast Guard Auxiliary. The idea took root in my brain to emerge twenty years later with significant consequences.

Dad bought a 1941 DeSoto car and it became part of a life–long memory when one of my buddies and I were driving it on Cadieux Road in east Detroit on Sunday afternoon, December 7th, 1941. We were listening to Glenn Miller big band swing music on the car radio. The station broke the show, and an announcer reported that the Japanese had attacked Pearl Harbor. I pulled over to the curb. We both were stunned, and suddenly aware our lives were going to change, and quickly.

Congress declared war immediately. We, as a nation, seemed to me to be so unprepared in the early forties and I remember the pride we all took in Jimmy Doolittle's air raid on Tokyo in 1942. *I would meet him personally twenty-some years later and would so tell him.*

As history unfolded, my December 7th pal was badly wounded on Iwo Jima as a Marine, pinned down for three days with legs full of shrapnel, and Glenn Miller died in an airplane crash in Europe over the English Channel. We were at war, as I had imagined we'd be.

My father had a strong work ethic and decreed that I get a part time job to help with home expenses and wartime prices. He wanted me to experience the thrill of receiving wages for work done. The first job I had was at a prototype of the modern supermarket. My task was stock clerk, moving groceries from cartons in the store rear to shelves out front. I learned merchandising and learned why vendors position their products so carefully. My second job was pumping gas at the corner station. It was a hot and dirty job but gave me skills in dealing with customers, minor repairs to cars, and watching the owner run his business. When I fuel up at our modern stations I often think about those days.

I wanted a job with a cooler and cleaner environment and I found one working at a haberdashery. I helped customers pick out shirts and ties, and even got good at selling fedoras, and my skill using the cash register had been noticed by the manager. One afternoon, he told me he had a medical appointment and said I was ready to close the store that night. I was so proud. It is still one of my fondest memories. As time progressed, my high school extracurricular activities increased, and my time for after-school work waned.

CHAPTER 3

BIG MAN ON CAMPUS?

Having navigated with As and Bs through the grades up to the tenth, at age fifteen I found myself as a freshman in a 4500 student high school, suddenly surrounded with scholars and laboratories. I joined clubs and activities, reluctantly accepting leadership roles, and studied hard in order to qualify if and when I had to go into the service of my country, in hopes for an officer commission.

Our homeroom, or study hall, was one of a set of three for boys. Ours had the unusual name of "House of the Twentieth Century Argonauts". We often wondered if someday a student named Jason would be one of us. The Golden Fleece seemed too ancient and mythical to matter to our young minds.

I enrolled in journalism class, an elective, and acquired an editorship on the school newspaper. At that early age, I learned the power of the written word, format of a good news story, the duty of a free press, the skills of headline writing, page layout, and most of all, the prevention of ambiguity in written and spoken language. The prevention of ambiguity was to become vital to my career later in my life as an aerospace launch operations engineer

In 1943, I was chosen by the student council to attend Wolverine Boys State at Michigan State College for a week of mock state government and there I was appointed editor of the daily newspaper published for the attendees. A graduate student advisor was assigned to give us guidance. His name was Jerry terHorst. Later in life he became press secretary to President Ford, then resigned that post in protest when Ford pardoned President Nixon after the Watergate debacle. Having been under his guidance for that week, I was not surprised at his action so many years later. At the end of the Boys State week when we arrived back in downtown Detroit we found the National Guard on full weapons alert, and a machine gun nest in Grand Circus Park. It was because of a race riot. It was hard for my idealistic young mind to comprehend.

Commensurate with my scholarliness, I realized my resume was lacking athletics, and after a short time as swim team student manager, I ran cross-country in an intramural track meet and was noticed by the varsity coach. My dream of being a jock became reality, and soon I was wearing the coveted varsity letter on a cardigan sweater with two-year arm stripes. That began my running and, like Forrest Gump, it never stopped, as I jogged well into my sixties. That action along with hiking and mountaineering built in me a heart, and lungs, that would carry me into my, at this writing, late eighties.

In my sports editor duties on the school newspaper, I met one of our football players. He was an unusual guy, quite studious, and never exhibited the jock mentality that was so common. He was kind, fair, and self-confident. Before we all graduated, I remember that he advised in his resume in the school annual (titled the Aryan, strangely, a word that later would signify Nazi racial arrogance) that his goal after graduation was to become a Lutheran minister. Years later, we would cross paths again, literally to my salvation.

Because our homerooms were alphabetically populated, I associated more with guys with names beginning in A through H. One of those closer friends took a leadership path into ROTC, a wise move in a war-active nation. He became a cadet lieutenant colonel. He was to later march across Europe as an army infantry captain, and most importantly, to come back into my life in a life changing way, when he brought to me my guardian angel.

The epitome of a typical teen's existence had arrived for me when I began the second half of my senior year, and some of my peers nominated me for senior class president. I began to think that I had it all; reasonable looks, athletics, excellent grades, journalism skills, and a cute blonde girlfriend. I was a shoo-in, I assured myself, to be elected. I felt like the classical BMOC (Big Man On Campus).

I remember the day well when they counted the ballots. I had been defeated, by a three to one ratio. I was devastated and was anxious to graduate just to escape the humiliation. I recalled my father's caution: "Never believe your own propaganda". In our final citywide cross country track meet we came in third and that glory was sufficient to see me through graduation day.

CHAPTER 4

YOU'RE IN THE ARMY NOW

Decision time was near as to a career path through the war. It was January 1944 and registration for the draft meant waiting to be called up to almost certain duty in the infantry. I decided to enlist as a seventeen year old in the Army Specialized Training Reserve Program (ASTRP). That put me quickly after graduation at the University of Wisconsin, enrolled, for six months, in pre-technical credit-earning curricula. Army advisors said our choices, and goals, after time there and after basic infantry training, were to be studies toward engineering, medical, or meteorology college degrees with officer commissions.

Now mid-year and the war on both fronts not going well, the days at Madison, Wisconsin were gloomy, the weather always seemed overcast, and even a visit by my girlfriend did not raise my spirits.

Then it was time to leave that campus and report just down the road to Ft. Sheridan, Illinois. After paperwork sessions, we received our uniforms and, on the second night there, were assigned to guard duty. We were issued old Springfield army rifles, for which we had no training. I was ordered to patrol along a half-mile fence, and yell "Corporal of the Guard, Post 4, All is Well" at intervals. After a hair-raising Jeep ride, I was dropped off at a dark intersection of camp roads and began my duty.

Then it struck me. On the other side of that fence were German prisoners-of-war, still wearing their North Africa campaign hats. I heard but failed to understand their catcalls in German. I saw that dreaded swastika again.

The war and I had met, for real.

In a few days I was on a World War I vintage troop train rumbling toward Camp Robinson, Arkansas with a few hundred other guys. The lights in the coaches were oil lamps. Soot was everywhere. The days were cloudy and wet. We were told that our destination was near Little Rock and that it was an Infantry Replacement Training Center (IRTC). Replacing who, and what, I wondered.

I began to understand now a little more about prayer, a God perception, and the meaning of life. My dabbling in various Protestant themes, and the study of Zen, Buddha, and Confucius were of little comfort. I needed a personal God. Where was he? Why was everything so depressing?

There was no relief at the IRTC, just more GIs, lousy chow, and rain and cold. Anxious to get into leadership and maybe a commission, I studied everything thoroughly. In weaponry, I shot expert in the M-1, carbine, Browning automatic rifle, and machine guns. I excelled in explosives school, and the bayonet. We were run through infiltration courses under barbed wire with tracer bullets flying overhead, marched through gas tents with masks off, and stood in muddy trenches for hours on end.

One day near the end of our training, we came in from a twenty-mile bivouac and were ordered at ease in the muddy company street, which was lined with wood-sided tents. It was drizzling and almost freezing. The first sergeant read off my name and a couple of dozen others, and we were told to report to the orderly room on the double.

The Battle of the Bulge had begun in Europe, and because I had shot expert in all the weapons, I just knew I was going early to the war because of my marksmanship, perhaps as a sniper.

The company clerk corporal, who could barely read, was trying to announce the orders in his hands and stuttered, "You guys are going to Virginia P . . . P . . . . Pol . . . Pol . . ."

I had thoughts of a special training site in Virginia for snipers.

Then one of our guys said: "Virginia Polytechnic?"

"Ya, that's it," he replied. We suddenly realized we were going to a college. It meant real school, that our ASTRP enlistment was still valid.

Then it hit us. Over in the company street, still in at ease stance, in the rain, were our buddies, watching us jump and holler. An instant realization came over us, and we quieted down and slithered out of sight.

We got a week's furlough and orders to report to VPI, a small military college in a quiet little town in Virginia's western mountains.

It turned out that the infantry company we left did not go to Europe but to the Philippines, and suffered 50% mortality.

The furlough at home was restful and revitalizing. I traveled anxiously by myself on a train to Roanoke, Virginia, and there took a bus to the small town of Blacksburg. There were instructions at the bus station as to where GIs should report.

We were assigned to barracks that the school, a military college, had used almost since the Civil War, and I soon was immersed in the electrical engineering curriculum. The army students were organized into companies, and the companies into battalions, and I was assigned the cadet grade of first sergeant for one of the companies. The purpose of the cadet grades was to maintain military discipline and allow the school military commander to have two battalions, one for the VPI cadets, and one for the army personnel. Here I was again, designated for leadership. I joked to myself as to whether I had a mark on my back.

The two battalions were designated a regiment and commanded by a VPI cadet as commander, and an executive officer, and an adjutant. Several VPI cadets were veterans who had already returned from combat in Guadalcanal and Europe.

My studies were intense, and rewarding. The professors were at their finest, what with the war objectives. My grades were excellent, and I was promoted (in the cadet ranks) to battalion adjutant. It was thrilling on parade day, every Friday, to call the companies in my battalion to order, and hear my commands echoing off of the buildings and nearby hills.

In mid-1945, one day I came into the barracks, and a group of guys were gathered around a visitor. He was a GI friend of one of our personnel. He told about being stationed at Oak Ridge, Tennessee on the Manhattan Project, whatever that meant. When pressed what he was doing there, he would only say "How would you like to have enough power to go to the moon some day?" His visit left us wondering all sorts of things.

It was soon evident what he had been doing. One sunny afternoon the radio blared with the awesome news that an atomic bomb had been dropped on Hiroshima, Japan, killing 100,000 Japanese. Little did I realize that within three years I would personally meet and talk with one of the scientists involved in that and future nuclear history, and later test giant rockets capable of throwing atomic warheads 5000 miles, and still later help guide satellites into earth orbit to detect such explosions.

And, never did I ever expect that 65 years later Hiroshima would be a glistening metropolis and my beloved Detroit a city in civil ruin.

Rising through the appointment ranks at the school, I reached cadet Regimental Executive Officer. It was the highest army cadet position at the school. VPI cadets held the two other regimental ranks. My position exempted me from marching to chow, and in fact, gave me the task of monitoring the drill excellence of the companies en route to the dining hall. I was also provided a seat at the commandant's table. For a brief time I pondered a military career knowing the Friday parades gave me a rush every time.

I visited VPI with my wife in the 1990s. VPI had become known as Virginia Tech and as a mighty university and the region was prosperous and built up. We walked to my old barracks site, and walked the old route to the "chow" hall, and out onto the parade grounds. I stood there in the midst of things, busy students hustling about, and remembered the sounds of my commands echoing.

President Roosevelt died in April 1945, and the observance at VPI that week is an event I never forgot. The cadence of the marchers, solemn music by the band, and tears of both soldiers and civilians were burned into our psyches. I felt so strongly the love this nation had for its fallen commander. It would take me years to undo that loss in my life.

I often ran cross-country among the nearby hills. One afternoon I was finishing the meet distance course in very fast time and up walked the coach, Gummy Proctor.

"Baldini, are you in already, gosh, man, good time." he exclaimed. "Say, how about coming back here after the war? I can get you a scholarship," he continued.

"I'll let you know, coach, sounds great," I promised. I never did let him know. Often I thought about what that future would have wrought.

In the closing months of my time at VPI, I received, along with two buddies, an invitation from Tau Beta Pi, the national engineering honor society, to accept membership therein. The initiation and banquet were very inspiring and I still carry my key with pride.

While I had spent 1945 in the safety of VPI, my male cousins, and my female cousins' mates, were serving around the globe in the navy and army. One of those mates was from Detroit's Polish neighborhood and because he could speak Polish he was assigned to an army unit freeing Jewish survivors at the Nazi concentration camps at Dachau. Years later I would hear him tell how horrible he found such places, and how much he despised the doubters of the

Holocaust. I recalled the revelations from Mr. Freeman, so long before.

When my time at VPI had come to an end, and as 1946 began, I was assigned to the Army Signal Corps as a grade T-4 (a specialist buck sergeant) to the Pentagon, to the 805th Signal Service Company, billeted at the South Post of Ft. Myers. There was an air of optimism and planning by everyone to fulfill their lives now that the long diversion had ceased.

I sometimes pulled KP duty there that GIs would fight for. The mess sergeant was an excellent chef and he catered to his KPs serving steak and eggs for breakfast, and lavish dinners, too. The Pentagon was a thrilling place to work, with generals and admirals galore. So many, in fact, that saluting was waived. Many times I held the door for a flag officer, or had one of them hold the door for me, saying "Go ahead, soldier". One of the generals I saw up close was the great Dwight Eisenhower.

Our unit's installation at the Pentagon was top secret and not declassified until 1985. It had been called SigSaly and was a pulse code modulation system that provided encrypted, undecipherable, direct voice communications between Washington, London, and the theater HQs. It was derived from that same technology demonstrated years before to me at the New York World's Fair. AT&T had brought it to the government to help win the war. The Germans and the Japanese were never able to decipher it and heard nothing but a buzz. It was nicknamed after a radio program called the "Green Hornet". After declassification, a set of the equipment was placed in a crypto museum near Ft. Meade, Maryland. Little was revealed in post-war years what importance that way-before-its-time technology had in the winning of that conflict.

The ASTRP program was closed and it was soon time for discharge, and I was processed out at the Pentagon, and went home now to Chicago.

CHAPTER 5

CHICAGO, CHICAGO

It was a day I remembered all my life. My train pulled into Chicago's Union Station and I boarded the elevated to the South 63rd Street station. It was a Sunday morning, and during the ride south I felt a normality I had not experienced in three years. The sun was shining. It was quiet. Arrival at my destination yielded an elevated station that was deserted. I stepped off with duffel bag on my shoulder and looked around for my parents, who were to meet me. Seeing no one for a moment, I felt a disappointment, then I looked down to the street level, and there stood my Dad, waving to me. I literally leaped down the stairs and rushed for the best hug I ever got from him.

"Welcome home, son, it is over", he said. I wondered how many parents had said that to sons and daughters over the last year.

The last five years seemed like a bad dream, a nightmare. Millions of earthlings had fought each other so violently to bring about a shaky peace after a plethora of "isms" had drugged mankind's brains. I wondered how long it would be before man would again be dragged into conflict and international criminality. It wasn't very long. Soon events in Korea would again begin to claim our youth, our resources, and our potential.

Shedding the khaki uniforms for post-war styles was liberating. I got a job downtown as a Marshall Fields department store stock clerk, and then as a men's clothing sales clerk. I was anxious to use my GI Bill funding, and my credits from Wisconsin and Virginia Tech, to finish college, and get a good paying job as an electrical engineer. I often reminded myself that I owed a debt of gratitude and service to my countrymen for a fine education.

With help from my father who had contacts at Illinois Tech (IIT), I was able to get into college there with only two and a half years of credits needed to get my electrical engineering degree. I immersed myself in the curricula and participated in the explosion of electronics applications that were a product of the war. I became interested in amateur radio and bought a shortwave receiver and logged stations from great distances around the planet. At IIT I was invited to join the Rho Epsilon radio fraternity and monitored the new single sideband voice communications mode between IIT (call letters W9YW) and Stanford's radio club (W6YX). One assignment I had there was to assist Marvin Camras, the man who had invented the wire recorder, and who laid the foundations for magnetic recording of all types.

I added to my life skills in writing and speech at IIT when I chose an elective course in semantics taught by the fabled Dr. Hayakawa. I joined the local chapter of my engineering honorary society and was elected treasurer. The president of the group and I became fast friends. In later life I was to meet him again, in a dramatic and historical space vehicle project, and still later when he became an assistant secretary of the air force.

One day a classmate and I were looking for items under the experiment benches in the IIT radio lab when we came across a box of two vintage television camera tubes, called iconoscopes. Television was still in its infancy and we were intrigued with the idea of building a TV camera. Not having the resources for all of the circuitry and components needed, we decided to cannibalize two RCA TRK-12 TV sets, which we found in the radio clubroom. We had no idea that the sets were from the 1939 Chicago World's Fair, and in the twenty-first century were to become very valuable.

We succeeded in our venture and the event would not go unnoticed at graduation time when job interviewers presented me with a career choice of lifetime importance.

In 1947–48 my choice of IIT continued to pay off. It gave me not only skill in television, but also the chance to work with the little used science of computers. Vannevar Bush, a famous MIT scientist of the time, was investigating mechanical differential analyzers. They were essentially mechanical analog computers composed of shafts, gears, differentials, and ball-and-disk integrators (as in mechanical speedometers). Output was written to mechanical x-y plotters. Dr. Bush had obtained a new machine for MIT and gave the old one to his colleagues at IIT. I was fortunate to be able to serve on the undergraduate support team for the researchers using the device. It was an unusual experience to get greasy working on an analog computer.

Commensurate with that activity, the electrical engineering faculty had persuaded Westinghouse Electric to donate an AC (alternating current) Network Analyzer to the school. This machine was an analog computer specifically designed to model electrical power networks for system stability solutions. My experience supporting the professors on that device also would turn out to be of great interest to job interviewers and present me with a difficult career path decision.

Amidst my studies, I was assigned a committee position for Honors Day, a senior event at the school, and my task was to pick up and guide the speaker for the day, and return him to his offices.

I received my assignment: Go to the famous University of Chicago stadium offices where atomic scientists such as Enrico Fermi were working and pick up a Dr. Edward Teller. I ventured into this secretive then, and famous now, area and experienced no unusual security. He was ready for me and seated himself in the car and we drove off toward IIT. He asked me about my studies, and then I had an opportunity to ask him about his experiences at Alamogordo and Trinity Site, and the first A-bomb test.

21

In his thick European accent, he said,

"We had on welder's goggles and we were all awaiting different results as to the pressures and all. When the countdown reached zero, I saw this little point of light lift up off of the desert floor.

I asked myself, 'Is this all there is?' Then I realized my glasses and decided to take them off. As I began to peel the rubber away from my face, the light pierced in, blinding that corner of my eye.

I said to myself, "Oh my God, what have we done!"

I don't recall his Honor's Day speech but I have always remembered the ride to and from that stadium.

Later in life, I was to meet him again. He would become known as "Father of the Hydrogen Bomb".

My time for career choice finally arrived, and I was offered an entry position at a consulting firm that provided TV station turnkey services. The TV station buildup in the nation was exploding and the demand for TV engineers was wide open. Meanwhile, the power company in Detroit was building an AC Network Analyzer, and wanted me to work on that project.

Despite the glamour and excitement of the burgeoning TV industry and the chance for meteoric rise into the networks and manufacturers, I chose the more staid and unique opportunity in the power industry, in my beloved Detroit.

I said goodbye to my folks and my Chicago friends and haunts, and left to begin, finally, my adult life.

CHAPTER 6

LOVE LOST AND FOUND

In Detroit, I had arranged to share an apartment with a graduating friend who went to work for Chrysler Corporation. After settling living arrangements, I was busy in my new job going through the engineer-in-training program at Detroit Edison. When that was completed I was assigned to the AC Network Analyzer project.

It was time for me to look up some of my buddies from the pre-war years. One of them that I was determined to meet again was the guy who had chosen ROTC in high school. He was living at home not more than a few miles from my apartment, and I found out his mother wanted to rent out a room and provide board. Soon I was moving in my meager belongings and enjoying her great cooking.

Efforts to date my high school steady girlfriend went nowhere and I decided that was a lost cause. It was actually fortunate for me because we had taken diverse life paths in education and interests. Besides, my work at the power company was going well, and I was pictured on the cover of the company magazine working on the computer project.

My boss was taking me with him to all sorts of technical meetings to show off the progress of this unique in-house project. I was his co-author for a technical paper about the machine, which was published in the electrical engineering journal. I really wasn't happy with all the attention because it meant more work. Nevertheless, hubris was creeping into my personality.

During that year, a doctoral candidate arrived at the power company. He had arranged to use the IBM customer billing punch card system at night to test experimental equations he had written for power plant efficiency. His work on that IBM equipment was an early indication of the use of digital computers. He did some minor tutoring with me.

I felt somewhat satisfied with my physical life but knew that my love, mental, and spiritual lives were, for the moment, wanting. I had no permanent home, was twenty-four years old, a bachelor, and with parents in another state.

One day my rooming host suggested I join him on a blind date. I stalled and hesitated for a couple of days and then finally conceded I had nothing to lose. He explained that my proposed date was attractive, educated, held a professional job, and was fun. The double date had been suggested by this girl's roommate, and their landlady was my friend's aunt.

The date night arrived and we used my recently purchased 1948 Ford sedan. I went to the door with him, prepared for disappointment in his glowing description and then we entered the living room where his date and mine were seated. I will remember that moment vividly for the rest of my life. I had the strange feeling that she was very special, the fulfillment of my dreams of a perfect woman, a one in a million match for my expectations. My prime activity for that evening was cautioning myself not to mess up this new acquaintanceship.

Her name was Jean and she was raven-haired, with a perfect high-cheekboned face and tall, beautiful posture. Her demeanor was sweet and polite and as the evening went on I sensed she liked my sense of humor, as she began to verbally jest with me. We went to a movie and later parked on their street. When my buddy and his date went into the house, Jean and I learned a little about each other's lives. My conclusion was that I had met a person of heartland American values, intelligent, glamorous, modern, and who was making more salary than I was.

I felt certain that my creator had sent one of his angels to watch over me. It was another of those moments of God-perception and it seemed almost magical. When the evening was over, she agreed to a date with me that weekend. I had fallen, for the first time in my life, truly in love. Delirious with the feeling, I was useless at work those few days, and could think of nothing but her.

Finally, the day arrived and I met her again. At second look, she was even more fantastic than the first meeting. We went to dinner at a roadhouse outside of the city. Her selection of clothes was perfect, and I felt so proud to have her in my company. Our dates became frequent and she decided she wanted me to meet her parents, and brother, who lived in a small town in Ohio. I felt gratified that I had gauged her correctly. Her family, including her war veteran brother, had down-to-earth values, and a conservative life style. On such visits I had the good fortune to learn the ways of small town America.

In the midst of this euphoria, I got a call from an army recruiter. My file had turned up in the U.S. Army Signal Corps enlisted records. The trouble in Korea and other communist-edged countries was requiring the army to staff up again after the World War II downsizing. They offered me an officer's commission. For an instant I was interested but then reality and the thoughts of separation from my newfound love shook me into turning it down. Then together we had months of fun, short trips, and outings with friends and relatives, and we began to talk of marriage.

Meanwhile, my career at the power company moved on, and the A.C. Network Analyzer was nearing completion. There were trips to institutions where my employer's engineers would run stability problems, and design new additions to the power company's high voltage systems.

It seemed to my love and me that it was time to marry. I bought a new cream Chevrolet convertible to further glamourize our upcoming ceremony and travels. Our wedding was perfect and our honeymoon romantic. My angelic bride was simply wonderful to be with. A week in a National Park, a trip into Washington, D. C., and visits to my grandparents and family displayed her poise and congeniality.

Soon, we were back and into a small one-bedroom apartment attached to a home along the Lake St. Clair shoreline. She continued to be my fabulous bride, always glamorous and chique, and interested in what I was doing in my hobby. She strove to cook, and keep house with my meager help, and continue in her exceptional career as a supervisory bacteriologist at a famous pharmaceutical company

One night in the winter of 1951, I stayed up late working on an electronics kit. The next morning I was sleepily ready to go to work, but not to drive. We both worked downtown near the same major Detroit street so she said she would drive while I napped going into the city. The route took us along the lakeshore boulevard. It was just thirty-two degrees, and I noticed a little ice sheen on the road. As we came around a highway curve in front of the Edsel Ford estate, we began to skid. The car swung around and slammed sideways up against the curb, striking an ornamental light pole. I had braced myself when the skid started, and after we hit the pole, it began to fall toward us. The vehicle rotated out from under it as it hit the curb. When I opened my eyes, my wife was not in the driver's seat, or in the car at all. My guardian angel had taken the brunt of the accident. I found her ten feet from the car, bleeding and nearly unconscious on the curb. In moments, we were being whisked to the nearby hospital. She was examined and found to have broken ribs.

Released after a few days to the regimen of healing, my mother offered to keep Jean at her place. About mid-week thereafter, Mom indicated that my darling had an undulating temperature and my mother's old world medicinal wisdom urged that our doctor's house call was in order. When he arrived and examined her, he ordered an ambulance to return her to the hospital. As they moved her from the bedroom, she fell into shock. Sirens were in order.

Outside the operating room the doctor briefed me. Her chances were about forty percent, he told me. Her spleen had been ruptured and she was bleeding internally. I remember nearly fainting at the thought. The terror of the moment remains with me to this day. I found myself waiting in the operating room anteroom, waiting for the movie-like entry of a doctor with a statement of the results.

The moment came, the bi-doors swung open and the physician announced,

"Well, we did one thing . . . ."

I waited for the terrible announcement.

"We saved her life. She will be OK."

I collapsed. I was weak, pitiful, sobbing, but thankful.

He was real now, that God that had been so elusive, who had just reassigned one of his angels to recurring duty on this planet.

This was in a time before seat belts, and I would recall this accident many times after I later had joined General Motors' corporate Engineering Staff. Not only did I watch a persistent engineer finally sell the seat belt idea to the reluctant heads at the company executive table, but also lose an engineer friend to a roll-over, sans seat belt.

My angel had healed after a time, so with her strengthened and my life at the power company settled into the norm, we set about fulfilling our commitment to population control, two kids. Jean knew that her professional career and motherhood would not be compatible and she accepted that, somewhat reluctantly. I will always consider her to have been in the vanguard of the women's lib movement. In due time, our daughter Anita was born, prematurely, but developed soon into a beautiful child.

We purchased a small bungalow in a suburban town. We knew we would miss the charm of the lakeshore life, the fishing, the fog, and the sush of the waves on the rocks, for this had been the proverbial American dream.

Then, and still today, I ponder how fortunate I was, how close the World War II Battle of the Bulge had come to my destiny, and on every observance of D-Day I mourn the thought of those American bodies frozen in the snow, washing up along Omaha Beach, and in the lagoons of the South Pacific.

CHAPTER 7

SEE THE USA

Being a new homeowner in a new housing development meant lots of landscaping, and furnishing. The typical American suburban life was fun and fulfilling, but my interest in the nearly complete analog computer had lessened at the power company. I had excelled in the electronics of the technology and was not at all interested in power company stability studies, so I set about to look for other employment. It was 1952 and everything seemed exciting and the economy was beginning to boom in reflection. The American Dream was emerging, everywhere.

We lived just a few miles east from a new ultra-modern campus that General Motors was building to house its Engineering Staff, Research Labs, and Styling Division. I investigated and found they were in need of an Instrumentation Engineer. I was hired at a better salary than I had been earning, and was working just a few miles from home in a thrilling new environment. I began singing every day the words to the new GM music "See the USA in your Chevrolet, America is asking you to call". War, armies, "isms", and civil strife seemed far off and irrelevant.

One afternoon Jean, our daughter, and I were driving north on one of the main roads near our town. We were passing a Lutheran church sign when I was startled to see the name of my high school friend as the pastor.

"He did, he did," I exclaimed.

My wife queried, "What are you talking about, who did, what?"

"My friend from high school, he said he'd become a minister, and he did," I answered. "I think we just found a church home," I continued.

The next Sunday we attended his church, surprised him and quickly enrolled, beginning a journey through Christianity that would continue for 55 plus years. From our studies under him, we acquired hope, faith and an integration of science with an almighty God.

At GM our department's job was to support the GM corporate Engineering Staff groups for power; transmission; suspension, and car Development. The assignments were challenging, and varied, requiring the latest instrumentation and electronics. I experienced ascendancy at my work place and was promoted to a managerial position that I accepted, of course, reluctantly.

My parents were anxious to visit Florida during the coming winter and so they were, along with the two of us, on the way down to the sunshine state when the Detroit winter began. We had left our daughter to stay with her grandmother in Ohio. I will always remember our first sight of a palm tree, and the warm sub-tropical sun replacing a frigid wind on our trip down. We all had a restful vacation, and after seeing everything from alligators to glistening springs, went home with wonderful memories. Our American Dream was real and we were reveling in it.

Back at work, I received word that we were to design exhibits highlighting GM engineering that would go on the GM Motorama auto show circuit of big cities, and that we would accompany them. The expression "it doesn't get any better than this" fit perfectly. With the exhibits built and tested, we were initiated into the business at the Waldorf-Astoria Hotel in New York City. The mix of glittering show cars, glamorous female models, and Broadway celebrities was almost too much for a self-proclaimed hayseed midwesterner like me. More so, we had some time off and caught the vibrancy of Times Square, Radio City Music Hall, and NBC.

The next stop was Los Angeles, and the preview night glittered with movie stars. I was assigned to escort three Hollywood stars and demonstrate the exhibits to them. One was the famous Jimmy Stewart.

My next assignment was Kansas City, and it was now summertime. It was an era of hotel window air-conditioners and the temperature seemed to stay above 100 degrees for days and days.

A year quickly went by and Motorama time was again upon us. With some new and some reworked exhibits on board, our first stop was the Miami show. I could hardly believe it, Miami in February. I sent my patient wife and darling daughter to her aunt's home in Ohio, while I, feeling guilt, emerged into the sunbaked Florida air.

After a somewhat sweaty show teardown experience, the boss called us together and said, "You can stay here on the company for two weeks, get your spouses down here, and have fun." I called my wife and told her to leave our daughter with her mother in Ohio, gather some summer clothes and fly down to Miami immediately. She executed those matters quickly and I was soon at the Miami airport picking up a gorgeous brunette in a flowery dress who looked as though she had just stepped out of the cover of Vogue. We then started a 10 day whirlwind tour of sights and nightclubs with my boss and his wife. Romantic dinners every night sealed the whole experience driving us madly more in love than ever. This was absolutely the American Dream and we were loving it.

This fantastic sojourn along with the memories of that terrible morning on the slippery ice, and the teasing lure of Florida during the trip with my parents were fueling our desire to somehow find a way to live in Florida. We wanted to experience the year-round romance and ambiance of the tropics, and the lack of winter. This trip was overwhelmingly romantic and addictive. We were hooked, but how to placate that lure?

Once back home, our interest in Florida was put aside for a while. We had taken the advice of our doctor, that my wife should consider having our next child (of the two we had earlier decided). So her pregnancy followed and our son, a ten pound, six ounce baby was born, his weight in contrast to his four pound, six ounce premature sister.

Returning home to a normal routine, it took some time to catch up on many postponed projects at work and at the homestead.

The Motorama had produced show cars like the Buick LeSabre, a long, low convertible with rakish design and fiberglass body. In my promotion I had reached the privilege of driving company cars home, ostensibly to put mileage on the vehicles prior to testing. We had the pick of the special garage, and one day I got the LeSabre. Driving on the main highway near home, the cops pulled us over to find out "what the heck car is this?" Our neighbors loved this practice and were always in our driveway at evening checking out the latest from GM's styling guru, Harley Earl.

One day prior to the 1953 Motorama later became historical for me. I was given the keys to, and drove home, a supposed future Chevy convertible. It was a very low, stylish body made of fiberglass but ugly in its unpainted status. I was to learn later that it was the original Corvette, fresh from the Car Development group's magicians. It was a Motorama hit.

Our engineering projects involved wear-cycle counters, transmission vane flow measurements, curved piston-cylinder pressure measurements and other automobile devices. Dynamometers and shake rigs populated the many test cells. Special facilities such as our copper-enclosed room provided an electrically quiet test environment. It all impressed me that autos don't just happen.

My experiences with the Suspension Development department in instrumenting the ride they worked so hard to perfect indicated that I was getting the data they wanted. The problem, they told me, was that the instrumentation was so heavy it was destroying the ride dynamics they were trying to achieve. They demanded I lighten up. I advised them I could use telemetry like the aircraft industry does. They OK'd the concept and we started to gear up. Months of learning and acquisition followed.

For a year or two during this period, I had become acquainted with a guy in Florida via amateur radio. He lived in Melbourne, Florida, and told me he worked on secret rocket projects. In our frequent contacts he was forever telling me of the idyllic life he lived in a sub-tropical paradise.

One Sunday my wife and I were at her cousin's house for dinner, lazily watching TV. Her cousin's husband was reading the Sunday paper.

"Hey", he said, "You guys are interested in Florida, aren't you, and here is what you said you were doing at GM. Telemetry Engineers wanted at Cape Canaveral Missile Test Annex", he went on.

"Give me that", I ordered. Sure enough, it was as he said.

"Call them up, see what gives", he urged. Quickly, I was on the phone to the recruiter at a downtown hotel.

After explanation of my career, the guy wanted to know when I could start! He guaranteed a better salary than GM but could not provide the stock bonus and company car provisions I had acquired.

Discussion with my guardian angel resulted in an adventurous decision.

"My God!"

"Florida."

"Rockets."

"Go for it."

CHAPTER 8

AND THE ROCKETS RED GLARE

The tentative employer set up a trip for me to fly to Florida, for interviews, and soon I was winging my way there. The company recruiter picked me up at the small Melbourne, Florida airport and I proceeded through a set of interviews at the Pan American World Airways offices at Patrick Air Force Base near Cocoa Beach, Florida. I was offered a position in Timing. I asked for time to consider. Before I left on the trip, I had arranged to also be interviewed by Convair. I was met at the gate to an Air Force installation called the Cape Canaveral Missile Test Annex. I had no idea, obviously, that one day mankind would leave this planet from this location destined for the moon.

The Convair man who met me told me, as we drove in past security, that he was a test conductor, one who manages the countdown and launches the missiles. We went to a Hangar J, parked, and he walked me in past two huge, stainless steel clad rockets with large rocket engines on one end. I tried not to look, as I knew this was a secret installation. He told me not to worry, because I was with him.

Here I was, here was war, again, now it was Russia, and the to-be-named Cold War. *What about the American Dream?*

I thought to myself. My peaceful life, in a sleepy suburb near mid-western Detroit, was going to change, big-time.

They wanted me, bad. The offer was the best yet, and I would be a telemetry engineer on an Atlas rocket launch pad. I was awestruck and hyper-excited. I committed that day to join them. I called my wife, and was soon flying home.

It was a frantic period, wrapping up affairs, putting our house up for sale, and attending good-bye dinners. My wife and kids were to join me after the house was sold. Nervous, actually scared, I started driving for Florida. As the miles ticked by, I became more and more apprehensive. *How would I ever hold my own with those rocket scientists and engineers?*

Arriving in the little town of Cocoa Beach, located right on the ocean, across a lagoon from Cocoa, Florida, I found a room and within days I was assigned to check out, and modify, the wiring of one of those huge rockets. I was assigned a crew of technicians.

On about the third day at my new location, I realized it was time for the weekly schedule with my ham radio friend. I found him on the air at the usual frequency and spoke carefully as though I was in Detroit environs. I asked him where he was located and I pretended to be looking at a road atlas, but was actually driving toward him. As I got ever closer to him, I made him describe his car, and then I pulled up behind him.

"Marv, this is W8ICN, mobile, in your rear view mirror," I gleefully explained.

He leaped out of his antenna-laden car and rushed to shake hands and asked for an explanation. That episode began several years of friendship, holiday dinners together and the like.

Some of the missile crew of technicians were really sharp guys who knew their electronics but others could hardly use a basic instrument correctly. I set about holding classes on instrumentation.

Soon the Base Manager decreed that each tech had to attend one of my classes.

We got the rocket ready and I was moved to a launch complex where the rocket had been erected in preparation for launch.

One evening, I had another one of those "I will never forget" experiences when I drove into the launch area Ready Room parking lot and saw that gleaming monster rocket erect and bathed in its service tower lights.

Now, whenever I see the Star Trek episode wherein Captain Kirk says "Sulu, take us out (Starship Enterprise out of the space dock)", and I hear that music, I recall with considerable emotion that night I first saw the tower moved away from the rocket.

Despite the daily phone calls with my wife back in Detroit, and my busy days, I missed her and the kids terribly, and was overjoyed when she told me the house had been sold, and that she had tickets for a flight into Orlando. I remember the day they disembarked from a turboprop airliner, at the Orlando airport. It was to, in later years, become an executive airport, replaced by one of the world's largest.

The scene at the airport was traditional, happy kids running to Daddy's arms, and Mommy passionately kissing Daddy.

We stayed at a variety of motels right on the beach, much to the kids' delight, awaiting the construction of our house in a development built for Atlas engineers and families. The company-sponsored housing was on a canal that emerged into the Banana River (lagoon), and was two blocks from the Atlantic Ocean.

Soon we moved in, frantically furnishing it with items bought in Orlando, the nearest city. We began a span of forty-one years of seaside living, boating, and fishing, coupled with travel throughout Florida. Awaiting me were, not only the excitement of rocketry, but also joining with sea captains and the U.S. Coast Guard in ventures, and partnering with some foot trail building visionaries in the Florida Trail Association. That would lead to meetings with cowboy ranch owners, and Indian chiefs, chopping through Florida's jungles with a machete, and led out state to the depths of the Grand Canyon and the ascent of Mt. Rainier. Access to the state's waters yielded events with treasure hunters, cruises of many of Florida's rivers, and the thrills of scuba diving in the pure waters of Florida and the Caribbean,

Our daughter, five years old, became a member of the first class of students that were to go from first-grade through senior high at the Cocoa Beach schools. Our offsprings were born in Detroit but they started out almost Florida "Crackers", remembering little of the big city.

It was summer, 1957, and the Cape Canaveral missile launch site had evolved from a long-range proving ground to a missile test annex. It was an annex to Patrick Air Force Base, Florida. The base, during World War II, had been a naval air base, Banana River Naval Air Station. It was famous as the base of the Martin PBM flying boats that went looking for the ill-fated World War II Navy Flight 19, of Bermuda Triangle fame. Twenty-five years later I was to meet a survivor of those tragic flights, my secretary's father.

A migration of rocket scientists and engineers was in motion from New Mexico's White Sands Range to the Cape. Germans, who the U. S. Army had smuggled out of Germany in Operation Paper Clip, made up a sizable contingent of those personnel.

At the Atlas missile launching pads, work was frantically proceeding in a race with the Soviets to test launch intercontinental ballistic missiles, the Atlas being the first candidate. I was working on the second rocket scheduled for launch.

One evening I was standing on an upper level of the service tower, the temperature was twenty-eight degrees and I was shivering in the wind from the ocean. Needless to say, I wondered if coming to Florida was a good idea.

I was watching the day the first Atlas lifted off. Not very long into its pitch over flight program, it exploded. Data suggested fire in the thrust section destroyed some electronics.

The pressure was now on our crew and after data analysis from the first launch, soon our missile lifted off and it exploded.

A "Tiger" team was called in to review the program. Among the members was the U. S. Army's Wernher Von Braun, the German who had been the V-2 project wizard. In quick fashion he reviewed the failures of the first two Atlas launches and advised that a fire shield was necessary across the rear of the rocket engine housing to keep rocket exhaust flames from destroying the engine compartment. Designs were changed and fiberglass heat shields and fiberglass cloth skirts for the engines were installed. The fix was successful and subsequent Atlas launches proved the design.

At that time I had no idea I would one day be in a first name acquaintanceship with Von Braun.

The pace of test launches remained frantic and the U. S., with a series of successes, felt confident.

During this period, Cocoa Beach was becoming known for its proximity to the missile programs. Visitors, especially engineers and technicians, were funding a boom in motel construction. Nightclubs and bars sprang up and the traveling men were funding illicit happenings. NBC-TV anchors Huntley and Brinkley dubbed our town "Sin City".

Unheralded were the resident families who were building a new community of libraries, schools, churches and businesses.

Then, on October 4, 1957, a small Soviet satellite named Sputnik crossed U. S. skies, beeping a simple tone. We all knew our lives would be changing again, big time.

President Eisenhower had already ordered the Navy to launch a Vanguard satellite, and now with the Sputnik launch, it was all the more important. However, the launch failed at liftoff and national morale was at a low point. It was then that Von Braun stepped forward with a satellite and rocket ready to go. They had been quietly developed under Von Braun's direction, dubbed Explorer I. Among those involved was Kurt Debus, Von Braun's Peenemunde launch site chief. Again, little did I realize that in a year or two I would develop a close relationship with that man and advise him during the beginnings of NASA.

The last years of the 1950s were historic almost every day. I was fortunate to be on the launch crew for Atlas 10-B. President Eisenhower wanted to follow up the Explorer launch with another significant rocket launch event. He wanted to assert America's expertise in space. His order began an unusually bold, and Hollywood-like chain of events that would make Sputnik look mere.

Vehicle 10-B was a typical rocket of the B group, a phase in the development of the final deployable Intercontinental Ballistic Missile (ICBM). It was erected on the launch pad and our team began the usual checkout. Then, quietly, under cover of darkness, odd things began to happen. The simulated warhead on the nose was removed and a lightweight aluminum cone put in its place. On the rocket's sides were pods holding various flight electronics. Some of the packages in those pods were removed and special canisters brought in to substitute. Being telemetry engineer on the team, I was especially suspicious when my systems canisters were removed.

As launch day approached, we all had deduced that the vehicle was being lightened and that the entire Atlas rocket was going to be put into orbit.

The countdown proceeded with eerie regularity and all systems were go, so our launch conductor pushed the engine start button and the bird, as we called them, rose into its supposed trajectory toward Ascension Island in the south Atlantic. Instead it went into low earth orbit. It was Christmas week, December 18, 1958, and fittingly, the huge rocket contained tape recorders and transmitters, turned on by signals from the ground, which began broadcasting President Eisenhower's voice wishing all mankind peace and goodwill. It was the first communications satellite, and dubbed Project Score.

Our boss had several copies of a special commemorative certificate printed on parchment paper. It listed the names of the crew, including my own. It remains a treasured possession to this day.

In developing the countdown procedures, we all became proficient when conducting such counts so as to never call a hold if we could figure a way to shift it to the Test Range. We were monitored by our bosses to insure that range time costs were not charged to our program.

The highways and roads of Brevard County, Florida had not been built with such a missiles and space boom in mind and so traffic jams were common. One of our local journalists rode in the traffic flow with a broadcast radio station link and advised about accidents, jams, etc. He later became one of great documenters of the space era, and an NBC commentator. I treasure the signed copy of his book I obtained years after his fame was secure in history.

Although the pressures of rocket launch schedules kept me busy, my wife and I worked diligently to enjoy the Florida life style. Because our home was on a canal connected to the lagoon west of the barrier island on which we lived, we decided a boat was in order. We purchased a wooden, varnished trailered runabout with a four-cycle outboard engine that was way ahead of its time. We set out to run up and down the Florida Intracoastal Waterway, docking at marinas and staying in motels. We began to see the lifestyle of the upper strata of society that reveled in yacht clubs.

We were also noting the number of unsafe and simply stupid troubles people on the water were getting into. One evening in 1960, while tuning across the amateur radio bands, I came across the Seventh Coast Guard District Amateur Radio Net, and found out about the U.S. Coast Guard Auxiliary. I remembered 1939 and my Dad's friend who had joined it then to help in the war effort.

I wrote to the Coast Guard office in Miami asking about membership. Soon I was teaching boating safety classes and formed a Flotilla in our part of the county. Weaving my rocketeering in with our boating became a skill I never lost.

My management skills began to gain notice and in the years 1960 through 1966 I served as a Flotilla Commander, as Division Captain of east central Florida, and as Rear Commodore of the Seventh Coast Guard District, comprised of Florida, Georgia, South Carolina and the Caribbean. Those years took our family to many rivers and bays in the District, each trip filled with camaraderie and good food with fellow members, and romantic nights with my beautiful wife. The Coast Guard activity was a welcome diversion from the pressures of the missile and space industry.

During this period, I had the special privilege to attend the National Search and Rescue (SAR) School at Governor's Island in New York harbor. It was an intensive one-week course by Coast Guard and U. S. Air Force instructors. I received its coveted patch and a new appreciation for the science in SAR.

Navigation training was available from the Coast Guard Institute, so I took courses in Piloting and Celestial Navigation. That knowledge was to later aid me one day when the Coast Guard issued us orders to go to the aid of a distressed boater forty miles out to sea from Cape Canaveral. Another member of the Auxiliary and I left Port Canaveral in his twenty-five foot cruiser on a calm day heading for the fishing grounds. Patiently I listened to his inboard engine chugging along at 12 miles per hour. We pushed along for 3 hours, heading out into the open ocean, with only water between us and Europe and Africa, and we finally came to the site of the "distressed vessel". It was a twin engine outboard that had some sort of fuel system trouble. Much to our displeasure there was another boat there, apparently fully operational. When he saw us, and our Coast Guard insignia, he promptly pulled anchor and sped off for home, leaving us to tow the fuel-less boat to safety.

I accounted for drift, and wind, and used bearings until I could see the high Kennedy Space Center structures to maintain a course home. We hit the opening to Port Canaveral right on the nose when it became visible on the horizon.

On the way out, we had to keep track of our fuel so as not to exceed the half-way point in fuel which if done would keep us from reaching home port. Also, the load of the towed vessel affected our speed over the bottom.

Obviously, we made it home.

CHAPTER 9

PRELUDE TO SPACE

In 1960, President Kennedy had not yet made his famous "to the moon" speech but the building blocks were falling into place. In the closing years of the fifties, the National Aeronautics and Space Administration (NASA) was organized and some of its cadre were chosen from the ranks of the Germans who had come with Operation Paperclip and were at the Army Ballistics Missile Agency (ABMA). While the Atlas and Titan ICBMs were being flight-tested by the US Air Force, ABMA and NASA were developing the smaller Redstone rocket.

Logically, key players in that endeavor were Von Braun and Debus. The former became head of the program and the latter was made Director of the NASA Launch Operations Directorate (LOD) at Cape Canaveral.

I had been promoted from Telemetry Engineer to Assistant Test Conductor on Launch Complex 11, and participated in many Atlas launches including the inertial guidance series. Many clips of memory include the time I was on periscope duty in the launch blockhouse and observed a fire in the thrust section of an Atlas rocket. When it finally exploded, I flinched away from the 'scope as though the debris would hit me and struck my head on an overhead beam. Another was when the hourly personnel, the technicians, went on strike. We

42

engineers actually checked out, and launched the missile. By late 1959, the four launch crews on ICBM Road were launching one Atlas rocket per week.

Project Mercury was begun in 1959 to launch astronauts into earth orbit. Walter Williams was named Director. He had preceded his Project Mercury post as head of the X-15 rocket plane program, working with the famous Colonel Chuck Yeager. Tom O'Malley was named Atlas launch conductor for the John Glenn flight. O'Malley had been my boss on Complex 11.

As the launch crew selections for the Glenn flight were being made, I was hoping to be a part of manned space flight history as an Assistant Launch Conductor under O'Malley. I wasn't chosen. Instead, I was sent to a new complex under construction, Complex 36, and handed the task of Pad Manager for completing the pad and launching the first Atlas–Centaur rocket. The Centaur was the first liquid hydrogen powered rocket in history with awesome weight-to-thrust ratio, and with a basic design that is still flying fifty years later.

The enormity of the task hit me immediately. Here I was again, reluctantly accepting leadership. The Air Force had been managing the program for the Advanced Research Projects Agency (ARPA) and was ready to hand it over to the fledgling NASA. The technology of handling liquid hydrogen was evolving at places like Pratt-Whitney in West Palm Beach, the Centaur engine builders; and at Convair's test facility in California.

Activities at the pad were plagued with instances such as these:

> On the first movement of the service tower to the launch pad, the tower was stopped six feet from its site because the designers had overlooked a diagonal steel beam that interfered with the umbilical tower. Cables and dead-men were used to hold the umbilical tower erect while fixes were made.
>
> During the first lowering of the Centaur stage onto the Atlas booster, the stages would not mate

because the mating ring and pins would not fit together. The cause was the factory was stenciling rings wrong by 90 degrees

On the Redstone contract, NASA-LOD, and its ABMA predecessor, had been accustomed to hands-on operations by their personnel with assistance from Chrysler Corporation. The contract that the Centaur designer and builder, General Dynamics, had with ARPA and the Air Force, called for delivery to the government after the contractor had finished and tested the rocket. A readiness review was then held for acceptance by the government.

As soon as NASA took over from the Air Force, the frustrations began to show in NASA system engineers, who could no longer touch their systems. My engineers complained to me about their attempted interference.

Finally, Dr. Debus called me to his office, where in several sessions thereafter, always after 5 PM, over pie and coffee, I disclosed to this veteran rocketeer how the contract worked. He took action and backed off his personnel. We became friends for the rest of his life.

Significant milestones in the handling of liquid hydrogen followed the mating of the Centaur. There were not, for the rest of Flight 1 history, any problems with the handling of this most elemental fuel, although thermal leak through the inter-tank bulkhead caused excessive boil-off during tanking tests.

The Atlas booster, 104-D, modified to boost the upper stage, checked out satisfactorily but design problems with the new upper stage plagued progress. Adding to the bulkhead problem were propellant slosh concerns, hydrogen embrittlement of metals, cracking of fiberglass hydrogen tank insulation panels and exceeding the number of times the thin tankage was "stretched".

During a program review at Huntsville's Marshall Space Flight Center in Von Braun's conference room, I briefed launch pad status to the group. I stated I would advise as soon as we, the contractor, were ready.

Much to my concern, Von Braun leaned forward and almost angrily advised, "Airnee, I tell you ven you are ready."

I quickly explained what I meant, and probably saved my job.

During 1960 and 1961, the program was under pressure from Von Braun. He wanted it cancelled so resources could be applied to the Saturn program. Nevertheless, he let things take their course and as 1962 approached, I was kept busy coordinating and participating in readiness reviews, both company internal and with the NASA customer. Convair had also been busy replacing program management in San Diego. One afternoon into my office walked the new Chief Engineer. I was shocked to find it was my old college buddy from IIT and its honorary engineering society chapter.

Replaced as Chief Engineer, Krafft Ehricke, one of the Germans from Operation Paper Clip, came to the launch base to say thank you to me for our team's support while under his direction. We spent several late evenings in my office talking about the future of space, satellites, and the like. He was a dreamer and conceiver, less a studied executive, but an excellent science-fiction author.

It was about this time period that I was visited by a fellow engineer who had left the Atlas program to work for a new company, at that time simply called the A company. He told me of the special reasons for the company and its special role in Air Force projects. I was interested in project work broader than just launch operations so I had an interview with his director.

The director implied I was being personally sought out for classified operations and that the job would be very challenging. Salary and benefits were way beyond what I was getting at the Atlas post. The thought of a more normal work schedule, and more time with my family, sounded great so I committed to join them after the upcoming launch. That company soon emerged as The Aerospace

Corporation, a high tech think tank and systems engineering organization, chartered by Congress.

Knowing I had a present task to complete as best I could, we held many rehearsals of Atlas–Centaur launch abort situations, and I realized that we should have all our drawings, and documents, in the blockhouse for launch.

Finally, it was launch day and we proceeded into a relatively smooth countdown. It was that time in the count when visitors were told to find their seats for the final period before liftoff. Seated at the launch conductor's console, I had Dr. Debus, KSC Director, opposite me, and my assistants and boss to my sides. Von Braun approached us, and I imagined he would deliver a short statement to us that the "stars awaited" or something spacey.

But, no, he said, "Good luck, Airnee, vee show doze Russians."

As the minutes ticked off, the tensions heightened, and just before my last poll of the systems and the test range, the public address system in the blockhouse was turned on. We had not rehearsed that and it startled me to hear my voice booming out inside that large chamber. I settled down and we reached T-18 seconds and I pushed the Engine Start button, the count proceeded under automatic control toward zero. I calmly placed my hand on the cutoff button and awaited the liftoff.

Suddenly, my ears were shocked with the word Cutoff! I pushed that button as hard as I could, even though the automatic systems had already performed the function.

I immediately, as we had rehearsed so many times, began to call for status reports from the systems console operators as to the status of their systems. Quickly, an unusual scenario began to emerge:

The umbilical booms to the Centaur upper stage, which were to retract just before liftoff, had operated in reverse, causing engine cutoff. We were left with only a range safety umbilical to control the rocket's electrical systems. All of the propellant and pressurization umbilicals had been disconnected so we were left with no way to detank propellants. That meant we had a load of liquid hydrogen, and liquid oxygen, and no way to remove the potentially violent mixture (used as fuel and oxidizer in the rocket's engines).

That also meant we had no way to keep the upper stage pressurized, other than boiloff of the propellants. Further it meant that, if we stayed in that configuration, the boiloff would eventually diminish and the .060 inch stainless steel tank would begin the collapse. To complicate matters, the electrical systems were now operating solely on the vehicle battery and if it ran down, we would lose control altogether.

I briefed everyone using the intercom system and PA, asked the visitors to remain calm, and then requested I be given a comm channel straight through to the Chief of Range Safety so that any safety decisions could be dealt with immediately.

The status looked grim until I was approached by the pad foreman, who announced that he had 10 volunteers willing to go down to the pad, secure the service tower around the rocket, insert the umbilicals, and get back. That would allow us to secure this sitting timebomb safely.

In the history of rocketry at Cape Canaveral up until that date, that was an unheard of request but I quickly relayed it to the Range Safety officer. He took no time at all to OK the operation, and the team proceeded, with all of our eyes glued on the TV monitors watching the team's every move.

Successfully, without incident, the team accomplished their operations and some eight hours later the launch crew secured the vehicle. Exhausted, everyone went home to rest before the next day's expected investigation procedures.

A pair of identical connectors in two cables on the umbilical tower had been crossed connected, even though we had run exhaustive timing test on the umbilical retract system and had secured the connectors with safety wire in their proper positions. Sabotage was suspected but investigation of that brought nothing conclusive and instant condemnation of such outrageous statements.

The next day one of Dr. Debus' project managers brought a letter addressed to me. It read:

National Aeronautics and Space Administration
Launch Operations Directorate
Cocoa Beach, Florida

M–LOD–DIR

Mr. E. A. Baldini
Centaur Test Conductor
General Dynamics/Astronautics
Post Office Box 999
Cocoa Beach, Florida

Dear Mr. Baldini

I wish, on behalf of myself and the other NASA personnel present for the Centaur launch attempt on April 21, 1962, to express my sincere appreciation for a job well done by yourself and the GD/A launch crew in returning the Centaur vehicle to a safe configuration after the launch abort.

Your conduct throughout the countdown, and especially during the period following booster cutoff when abort procedures were necessary, maintained order in a situation that could easily have been chaotic.

You are to be commended for your display of calm professional leadership under extremely trying conditions.

Very truly yours,

Kurt H. Debus
Director
Launch Operations Directorate

When I got home that night, and after I had told my wife of the unbelievable day I had, I decided to write my parents about the events.

Dad had risen to become Plant Manager of a Chrysler auto assembly plant, but a new wave of younger Chrysler executives marked him for retirement. It was part of their plan to bring in new talent to staff the company. After Dad retired he signed on with a consulting team and he and Mom went to Calcutta, India on a consulting contract. His mission: to assist Hindustan Motors, an Indian government initiative, to develop a national automotive manufacturing industry.

It was an exciting move. They were set up in a house in Calcutta, and were supported by eight servants. Mom had only to ring a bell to be assisted in any household matters. While Dad struggled to get the Indians to accept newer ways of building cars, Mom busied herself by joining the American Women's Club, assisting no less than Mother Theresa herself. Mom saw the unfairness of the caste system but never tampered with it in the open. On one occasion they took a holiday with the Women's Club to Darjeeling at the foot of the Himalayas, There at a dinner party hosted by the club, they met and talked with the guest of honor, Sir Edmund Hillary. He was in the region working with the Sherpas on educational and conservation projects. As I sat to write of my day's excitement, I reread a letter from them in which they were hinting that the next consulting job was to be in Japan.

With investigation of the Centaur launch attempt now completed, the rocket and pad were again readied for launch. My airframe engineers complained continually about the fragility of the Centaur hydrogen tank insulation panels. It seemed that every time the panels were handled, the team would find cracks in the fiberglass structure, which was used to enable helium purge of the space between the tank wall (at 325 degrees below zero) and the panel. Despite no-go opinions by me, and members of my team, the company recommended to NASA that the vehicle was go for launch.

And so, on May 8, 1962, Atlas-Centaur F-1 was launched, after the booster stage had been on the pad for over one year. The liftoff followed a fairly smooth countdown, with built-in holds, and began its programmed pitch toward downrange. At Mach 1, fifty-five seconds into flight, with maximum dynamic pressure on the airframe, the Centaur exploded, the Range destroyed the Atlas and the wreckage plummeted into the sea. Investigation followed and the conclusion was failure of the insulation panels, with Centaur tank fatigue from too many stretch cycles as a secondary cause.

Soon after this event, Astronaut Scott Carpenter's Project Mercury launch was imminent over on Pad 14. I was called to a meeting to determine what to release to the press about the Centaur failure's relationship to the Mercury Atlas. There were just four of us in the meeting: John Glenn, Dr. Hans Gruene (Deputy Director of KSC), Lt. Col. Mullady (USAF), and myself. Glenn showed his leadership traits well in that session, and we soon had a well thought out statement that showed the Centaur failure had no relationship to the Mercury Atlas rocket's integrity.

It was awkward to be leaving after a failure and I felt somewhat downhearted about departing what I still believe was one of the best launch teams ever assembled.

Dr. Debus heard of my leaving and personally called me to come with him, instead of Aerospace, to take a position in the Saturn Project Office. Hmm, I felt a tinge of history pulling at me, the moon program, but I told him I had made a commitment.

Then, on the tail of that offer, came one from Bob Gray, legendary head of the NASA Unmanned Launch Operations Directorate, for me to be the local NASA Centaur Chief. I declined that offer, reluctantly, as I liked Bob.

And so the Centaur chapter ended for me, but not for the vehicle. As the years went on, the problems were cleared and she became the workhorse of interplanetary launches and the commercial satellite business.

At this very moment, the Voyager spacecraft, powered into Earth escape trajectory by a Centaur in 1977, is just now leaving the solar system and entering interstellar space.

One day in the closing months of my Centaur activity my girl cousin in Virginia called me and screamed into the phone, "I saw you in the movies, in the movies!"

After I calmed her down, I found she had seen *Angry Red Planet*, a science fiction movie produced by Hollywood that had used clips from a USAF documentary. I acted as a Launch Conductor of a typical Atlas launch in the USAF film but it appeared in the movie version as Landing Conductor of an Atlas returning to Earth from Mars. The three-second clip showed me wipe my lips and adjust my glasses in anxiety as the ship settled into its landing fixture. The producers achieved this appearance by printing the original film of the lift-off backwards. In later years, I found and kept a video of the film.

CHAPTER 10

CONSOLE TO DESK

I had left the grueling job of life at the launch pads, the long hours, hardware hassles, manning of consoles, and ears sore from headsets. It was exciting but repetitive, challenging while boring, but all of the time it had been a privilege to work with terrific people that gave me so much support, loyalty, and high performance. It was now mid-1962 and I was leaving that for the more routine life in a project office, with the stacks of paper, endless telephoning, countless meetings, and briefings, and several dozen airline flights, but with time for family with more stable hours and more vacation time. While my career life was changing, so was my personal life, especially time to get into the Florida life style, and to fall in love again with my wife, who was becoming more maturely gorgeous every day.

Upon my arrival at Aerospace in June, I was assigned as Aerospace's launch base project manager for the Vela Hotel program, designed to detect and measure nuclear detonations in space. The spacecraft was built by TRW, the upper stage Agena by Lockheed, and lifted off by an Atlas. My integration skills fit well with program needs and we had a successful launch. The previously unseen radiation background data from the satellite interested Aerospace scientists and they called in the famous Dr. Van Allen. In cooperation with the Sandia Labs people, data analysis revealed a plot of the solar wind never seen before. We all felt we had contributed greatly to the understanding of our planet's basic environment in the solar system.

The U.S. Air Force colonel who was Vela Program Director, when learning of the promotion of the Aerospace Vela Program Manager in Los Angeles, suggested me as the replacement. My management had other ideas about me.

Meanwhile, General Electric Company was looking for a new Base Manager at Cape Canaveral and KSC. I was approached and offered a very attractive package. In a sudden career moment I told them, without much analysis or soul-searching, that I would accept. After a day or two of admonition by close friends and family about my commitment to Aerospace, I had to call and take back my acceptance. They were courteous about it and asked who I would recommend. I gave them some candidates' names and closed the subject with them. As I reflected on my actions in the months that followed, I realized I had not done my reputation any good. My hubris suffered a big setback that day.

My doubt about my career move was further erased in 1963 when I was called to the Los Angeles office of Dr. Walt Williams, now an Aerospace Vice President, and former NASA Chief for the X-15 Rocket Plane, and past Operations Chief for Project Mercury.

He told me I was to be the corporate contact at the Cape for certain classified programs due to be launched there, and also that the Air Force was developing a manned program, called the Manned Orbiting Laboratory (MOL), in which he wanted me to take a strong launch management role.

During that trip I had the good fortune to be in a briefing to the Board of Trustees about the above. Jimmy Doolittle was among them so I got a chance to meet him and briefly tell him how much he meant to all of us for his daring in World War II.

I was given the name of my local contact at the Cape and together we began to setup what was the forerunner of the National Reconnaissance Office (NRO) operations at Cape Canaveral.

To add to the mix, I was promoted to Projects Director with a staff of engineers managing Aerospace's efforts on all of the military spacecraft projects at the Cape. This time my ascendancy felt a bit more comfortable because I had a great staff and I had a challenging task ahead.

Integration of the component stages of a military launch vehicle became a focused expertise of my group. Test flow rationale had to be flawless and reliability high, as each payload's cost approached a billion dollars. We kept the big picture in mind, and got very good at looking for trouble, or false trouble, at the interface between rocket stage contractors, and between them and the spacecraft contractor.

Examples of non-problems such as these were evidence we had the big picture viewpoint:

After the Navy's first FLTSATCOM spacecraft passed a perfect systems test in the Satellite Assembly Building it was taken to the launch pad and mated it to the launch vehicle. When the Aliveness Test was run, the spacecraft contractor reported spurious signals in the passband of the spacecraft's radios. One of my engineers reported the problem to me. I asked if anyone had listened to the signals. He pondered that question and asked why I asked it. I suggested to him that because the antenna couplers had been removed at the pad the spacecraft was probably hearing the signals it was designed to pick up, namely UHF radio. He called me back later and told me that was the reason and that all was well.

On another launch vehicle we had cautioned the upper stage contractor to use the booster's flight and ground test guidance signals carefully because those signals were sent in different time spacing during ground test than during flight. When I came into the launch complex ready room to meet with my program manager from Los Angeles, he reported the flight systems test discretes from booster guidance were off by seventy seconds. I told him the system was fine because that is the difference between the guidance discretes ground list and the flight list. He immediately took off for the blockhouse to tell the contractors what they had overlooked. After that episode, he always insisted that I, or my team, check all such procedures.

The reputation of my team began to permeate through to the various contractors' factory test people and especially those responsible for testing at the launch base. Also the local contractor reps started to work closely with us, seeing us as agents for their good.

Programs were stacking up and my work on classified programs was hindered by a limit on the number of engineers that could be involved in those programs. The load was beginning to tell on me and my Florida lifestyle was taking second place, although I remained actively engaged in Coast Guard Auxiliary work.

We began to know more about each contractor's test equipment commonalities between programs than the contractors' own engineers did. We would look for a known problem in the contractor's Program A after seeing it happen on that same contractor's Program B, while the contractor's Program A engineers were kept by security from hearing about it.

My life during these years was filled with the excitement of taking part in the development of highly advanced near-earth space technologies. Meetings were often classified and I repeatedly had to fly across the entire country for a one day three hour meeting to settle an important test issue or make a status briefing to program managers. Destinations varied and when schedules allowed I would take time to hike any nearby trails or mountains in that area.

Among the many programs in my Cape responsibilities list was the now famous Global Positioning System (GPS) which changed the science of navigation forever. My staff engineer and I were able to influence the launch base checkout and launch procedures such as to produce high launch rates and rapid response to calls for launch.

The MOL program was developing quickly and we had to learn about manned spaceflight launch operations in just two years to launch. We began monitoring NASA operations at the Cape and the results of Projects Mercury and Gemini. The Titan 3 launch vehicle was chosen to boost a refurbished NASA Gemini spacecraft (dubbed Gemini II) on a downrange suborbital flight. The flight objective was to test a modified reentry heat shield, with a cutout in it, for a to-be-designed hatch for the astronauts to crawl through. A Titan propellant tank was used to simulate the MOL.

We quickly established good working operations with the Gemini spacecraft engineers, and earned their respect with suggestions about procedures and test flow. The robot astronauts that were to fly in the vehicle caused just enough procedure changes to require detailed scrutiny.

Soon it was time for final acceptance of the space vehicle at the factory by the Air Force. Our USAF-Aerospace team arrived at the factory feeling somewhat inadequate to question the veracity and experience of both the contractor and their NASA in-plant experts.

As we inspected the vehicle everything seemed meticulously in order until I traced the installation of the steel cable that attaches the capsule to the parachute cable. It appeared that the cable, when operated, would tear an electrical cable from its mountings. We felt we had to be wrong in our observations and were very reluctant to report this to NASA. However, we knew we were literally required to do it.

When we advised the contractor and NASA team about it they were astonished and chagrined and called an immediate meeting to determine the cause of the error and its immediate correction.

Needless to say, we quickly became qualified members of the team.

The MOL launch preparations went well, and we thrilled in checking out experiment packages inside the Titan tank, pretending what it would be like in a weightless state inside the cavernous enclosure.

The launch went very well. We operated a small Control Center and with the Navy's help recovered the capsule safely.

Meanwhile, the program planners in Washington were having second thoughts about the need for the program, i.e., manned reconnaissance vs. robotic reconn. The latter prevailed and the program was cancelled.

My activity in the Coast Guard Auxiliary heightened during this time period and I was selected to the office of Seventh Coast Guard District Commodore. Responsible for the Auxiliary in Florida, Georgia, South Carolina and the Greater Antilles and wearing a star on my shoulder boards, I felt the heavier load. Compensating for that was the onset of adventure, travel, romantic interludes with my wife on Caribbean islands, and a chance to make the Auxiliary more valuable to the Coast Guard. Further, my association with local mariners expanded during this period.

Because of the Auxiliary, I met and talked with another celebrity, a great documenter of the twentieth century, Walter Conkrite. It happened at an Auxiliary National Conference where he was to receive Honorary Commodore designation. At cocktails before the award dinner, I found him momentarily alone in the midst of the attendees, and took the chance to meet him.

"Mr. Conkrite, sir, a good friend of yours is my boss." I said.

"Oh, who is that?" he queried.

"Walt Williams. Your old space buddy."

"Gee, how is Walt, we spent so many good times together during Mercury launches at the Cape."

"Yes, he is at The Aerospace Corporation in L.A."

"Here, let me hold your drink while you write that down for me."

We chatted for a few more minutes and we parted as he said "Thanks, Ernie. Be sure and tell Walt hello."

My Auxiliary rank had placed me on its National Board at a time of rapid change. Besides voting for uniforms with a more Coast Guard appearance, I had developed a U. S. Coast Guard Auxiliary

Officers Manual for the Seventh Coast Guard District that had become a model for other Districts. I had convinced the Coast Guard in our district to allow Auxiliary radio operations on Coast Guard VHF–FM Coast Guard channels. It was very successful and became the model for a national setup.

These activities put my name into prominence as a candidate for National Vice Commodore, a position usually reserved for the next in line National Commodore. This was not to be for me, though, because my peers on the Board felt my space industry responsibilities would keep me from adequate attention to full time office and so I was not chosen. Secretly, inside, I felt the fear dissolve away when I heard the news.

My years after that yielded great experience on the National Staff as editor for training texts in Search & Rescue, Piloting, and Communications.

Chapter 11

Time and Space for God and Family

Our spiritual life was never lacking during these years of our lives. In 1960 my wife and I became part of a Lutheran mission congregation in Cape Canaveral, Florida. We held offices in the church, Sunday school and the women's group. It was a time when Cocoa Beach grew in population. Before we built our permanent church building our mission congregation used a local cocktail lounge for a church space. Saturday night's liquor glasses and full ashtrays had to be removed early Sunday mornings.

My wife and I were responsible for the cross and communion ware. We kept it in the trunk of our car. One night, coming off of the Cape, it was my time to be checked by security, for pilferage. The guard asked me what I had in the trunk. I whimsically said, "A church."

He responded, "OK, wise guy, out of the car, and open the trunk."

I opened the trunk, and there in proper position to make full visual impact was the heavy wooden altar cross.

He blurted, "Ah, ahem, excuse me, sir. Be on your way, sir."

When time came for our congregation to write a constitution, and by-laws, and such, the skills of its spacemen members came to great value. After writing contracts, statements of work, and budgets, in jobs at the Cape it was easy to fulfill the church duties needed.

The pastor of our flock was proud of the spacemen in his congregation and boasted to his pastor friends "Where else can you have a member shoot a multi-million dollar rocket on Saturday and teach catechism on Sunday?"

These spacemen were always able to explain quite directly how they made their religion relevant in the midst of so much technology.

This came to fruition for me in a very special way. I taught senior high boys in the Sunday School. Their questions at that time in their life were full of what seemed like conflicts between science and the Bible. Somehow, with divine guidance and my own God-view, we together built an understanding. I was very pleased to learn in later years, that one of the boys earned a doctorate in geophysics and became a NOAA scientist and President of his congregation; another became an M. D. and President of his congregation, and another became a Lutheran minister.

One Sunday morning we came into church, sat down and opened the bulletin. On the back was a facsimile of a letter with NASA letterhead that read:

Dear Pastor,

Thank you for your invitation to worship with you when I am in Cocoa Beach. Usually, I am not there on weekends but when I am I worship at Riverside Presbyterian.

I will consider visiting soon.

And please give my regards to Ernie Baldini.

Sincerely,
Wernher Von Braun

The pastor had written this without mention so it came as a surprise to me. I was very pleased that Von Braun would remember me, and that the pastor mentioned my membership in his invitation.

In some later year, I asked the pastor for the original letter so I could photocopy it. He sheepishly confessed, "We can't find it."

The pastor died not knowing what a valuable piece of paper had been lost.

On a flight home from L. A., I sat next to a man in a tailored suit. He noticed I was reading a technical magazine and began conversation, asking, "Are you an engineer?"

I answered in the affirmative.

He began to ask questions about my faith and about conflicts he had found between the Bible and science. I explained several ideas that reconciled the problems I had been through with the same. We talked for almost two hours.

When he left the flight at Dallas, he asked me "Is it OK if I use some of your thoughts in my sermons?"

With an astonished gulp, I gave him permission.

Relief from the grueling schedules of the early sixties gave me time to consider the needs of my family. I wanted the kids to see their great country, to learn what is out there, and to do it early enough in their lives to assist in their living and learning. My employment at Aerospace included three weeks vacation per year and could be saved up to ten weeks total. Our plan was to buy a tent and camping supplies, and tour out west across the South, Texas, the Southwest, California, and then east across Nevada, Wyoming, and down through the Midwest to home.

We had a 1963 Pontiac station wagon and took off on a six-week trip in the summer of 1964 with tent atop the car. Alabama and Louisiana were rainy, but Texas was dry. That was a recipe for a shrunken tent by the time we opened it in dry, hot Texas. In New Mexico the kids experienced their first look at western mountains, and their first bear in the ice chest. Next they stood in awe at the

Grand Canyon. In a campground at Boulder City, I happened upon a coworker from Florida. We all four marveled at the Golden Gate Bridge, wondered about Alcatraz prison, and held on to our money in Reno. By the time we arrived at Yellowstone, the New Mexico bear had also (he came north on the Continental Divide), and he robbed our ice chest a second time.

This trip settled deep in the minds of our children and they still talk about the great times we had in that six-week excursion.

CHAPTER 12

How High the Moon?

During the period leading up to the MOL launch, I was also very busy with the classified programs launches. By 1967, we were all watching the quick pace of the moon program.

Apollo 1's capsule was being tested in preparation for the first launch. In a horrific instant, three astronauts were killed in a capsule fire. The NASA Chief Spacecraft Test Conductor was my neighbor and was manning that console during the fire. He later became NASA Space Shuttle Launch Director, and then Deputy Director of Kennedy Space Center.

Program investigations resulted in hundreds of programmatic and personnel changes. One of those was a directive from NASA to North American Rockwell to hire Tom O'Malley, my old boss from Atlas days, to head up their operations at KSC. O'Malley was a tough manager who successfully ran the Atlas operations on Project Mercury and was stationed at General Dynamics' submarine plant in New England.

When I heard that he was coming back to the Cape, I told my wife that I would get a telephone call as soon as O'Malley was back in town. Sure enough, the first day or two of his arrival, he called.

"Ernie, I want you to come and work with me on Apollo."

I asked "Doing what?"

"I want you to be my Capsule & Service Module Test Manager". He replied.

I thought for a moment, *gosh, the moon, it would be my ship that was going to the moon.* I was excited and told Tom I would tell him after the weekend.

This was another fork in my career road. Here I was, a vital cog in the launch operations of defense and intelligence satellites responsible to the highest levels of government, tempted with a history-making management position in mankind's greatest adventure. My family and I knew the sacrifice in time it would place upon me, and how it would affect our marriage, our family experience and my health. We concluded together that I was already serving my country diligently and so on that Monday morning I called Tom and told him I had a high-level commitment I just had to keep.

As the years went by I forgot about the nearness of great history to my door, and it was only on one day that I regretted that decision. It was the moment when Neil Armstrong began his phrase:

"That's one small step . . . ."

"How High the Moon?" became my wife's and my favorite song, and it crystallized our commitment to each other as nothing else could have.

I did not realize but one more career change challenge was ahead a decade later.

While this was transpiring, my parents had finished their stay in India, and then went to Japan to the Nissan automobile company. Dad was so impressed with his Japanese customers that he wrote saying, "These guys are very good, someday they will take over the world car market."

He achieved great success in his consultations with the Nissan engineers before returning to the states. His career ended suddenly when he died of lung cancer (two packs of cigarettes per day for forty years) in 1967 at age sixty-seven.

In Dad's final years I realized how really intelligent, industrious, and skilled he was. While not a college graduate he had learned the equivalent by his International Correspondence School studies. His politics, world-view, religion, and friendship, were admired by all of his peers. I will remember always his saying "Don't believe your own propaganda."

A few months after Dad's death, my mother moved to Florida and lived in a high-rise near our town for twenty-three years.

My parents had lived an American dream.

CHAPTER 13

VOLUNTEER IS A VERB

1970 was a marker in my life for it was when I found the Florida Trail Association (FTA). Hiking had always been a fun thing to do, and our family had day-hiked many of the National Park trails of the eastern U. S. One day in July I was reading the Florida Sportsman magazine that had an article about the association and the man, Jim Kern, who started it, with the idea of a foot-trail the length of Florida.

I mentioned the article to my wife, and she suggested that backpacking on the trail would be fun, and emphasized we had hiked before, why not overnight? Within a day or two, I was at Sears grabbing up the necessary gear to try a trip on the Florida Trail in Ocala National Forest. What we didn't know was that you don't backpack in Florida in the summertime. My family was brave and we made it through but it wasn't until a year or two later we realized the dangerous folly of our adventure in that summer heat.

Our membership in the FTA yielded the knowledge that Florida's hiking season was October to April. I thought that was great because you could have a yearlong schedule with northern and western trips from May to October and on the FT in the winter.

We soon learned the basics and began to sign up for Appalachian Trail trips and winter backpacking on the FT. For me it was a great counter to the stress of the rocket and space industry and I cherished the chances.

In 1974, I signed an FTA volunteer postcard and found myself assuming the role of Cartographer of the FT. That was the beginning of many wonderful years in the natural beauty of the Sunshine State. I learned a new appreciation for the precious commodity of clean water, the horticulture of tree farms, the changing landscape of rural America, and the miracle of the light switch. The lessons our children learned on the trails, I would realize later, helped them face life directly with wisdom and courage.

In the conferences and meetings throughout those years I forged a lasting friendship with Jim Kern, and many other wonderful people. At the time this all began, I had no idea I would wield a machete in Florida's jungle, negotiate with tribal chieftains, and ride with real cowboys.

For fifteen years I scouted or mapped routes of the trail. The digital age had not yet arrived so maps I made were paste-ups of Florida Department of Transportation maps. My family and I spent many days scouring property maps in county courthouses, and checking fences, and bridge crossings. Most of the property owners we encountered were fine citizens and willing to help as long as their property was not endangered.

My wife and I had a chance to meet a legend in Florida history, Marjorie Stoneman Douglas. She was 100 years old when we met her and she signed her book, River of Grass, for us. It was about the struggle to save the Everglades. She was the main speaker at a FTA meeting I chaired and it was awesome to watch that centenarian stay on subject and speak with vigor.

Along the way through those early days, I met Ross Allen, a famous Floridian herpetologist who had set up the first serpentarium near Ocala.

While scouting for the trail's route through the Seminole tribal lands north of the Everglades, we visited Chief James Billie's office in Dania, Florida. He was enthusiastic about the idea and promised support. While in his office, I noticed a picture above his desk showing him (I guessed) wrestling an alligator. When I asked he acknowledged it was and said, "One day at a Florida (Gators)-Florida State (Seminoles) football game, in a half-time show, I wrestled a gator to the ground, and the fans went nuts. It was my greatest moment."

The efforts of thousands of Floridians were building an exceptional natural asset for the people of Florida, and I was proud to be a part of it.

Meanwhile, at the Cape, the Air Force commander for our missions and operations transferred to Vandenberg Air Force Base in California. After settling in, and surveying the management of our company operations there in support of the Air Force missions, especially the classified ones, he wanted me to head our operations there.

He directed the Air Force contracts people to set it up and Walt Williams was soon on the phone to me seeking my acceptance. It meant leaving my beloved Florida, it meant the kids would be detached in the midst of their college years, and it meant an awesome challenge, and opportunity for me.

We considered the higher cost of living in California. We realized that living in, say, Solvang, could be a wonderful setting. It is a Danish village type of town.

We decided we would go, but for a minimum of a twenty percent pay increase to cover the increased cost of living in California *(and to overcome my fear and reluctance)*.

The company response took no time at all. My requirement did not play.

I often still think about the ambiance of California living, the quaintness of Solvang, and wonder if that move would have led ultimately to a transfer to our Los Angeles headquarters. Smog, traffic, and taxes, I always concluded, were not for me.

During the lazy days of the summer of 1972 my interest in professional football was piqued by news reports of an impressive NFL Miami Dolphins team. The Sunday and Monday night games were a nice interlude against the rocket urgency of each week. I began to read every sports column and digest to learn more. It seemed that the Dolphins franchise had assembled, in my mind, a near perfect balance of talent, coached by a skilled master of the game. It was one of those times in your life when you think you really understand something very clearly.

I carried this feeling into the office at the Cape one day, boasting, "I think the Dolphins can go all the way this year."

"You mean undefeated?" a USAF colleague queried, "Are you nuts?"

"Seriously, I believe they can go lossless all the way and win the Super Bowl," I said.

"You're on," my friend shot back, "What do you want to wager?"

"Dinner in Orlando, $50 minimum," I confidently responded.

"Fine," he closed our discussion and left the scene.

The preseason came and the Dolphins had an average run of wins and losses, and I was sure I had shot off my mouth again, and would pay dearly for it. Every Monday or Tuesday morning he reminded me of my stupidity. Then the regular season started and the number zero in the lost column wasn't changing. I remained civil and quiet for a few weeks but then I began to ask him if he wanted out of our bet. He remained confident and ignored me. To make matters worse for me, the Dolphins quarterback was injured and out for the season.

By December, he was complimentary of the Dolphins but kept saying they would meet defeat. By playoff time, I was in awe at the team's performance and knew in my heart they were going to do it.

By Super Bowl time, I was not on this planet. I could not believe what was happening. When the game ended, I acted like a child with a new toy. I jumped and hooped and hollered.

My friend and his wife cordially bought us a deluxe evening at an expensive Japanese steak house.

All of our colleagues at the Cape knew of our bet and my calling it right but no one, no one, reported it to the media.

At this writing, forty years later, I am still waiting for even a Super Bowl, with losses.

THE ASCENT OF MAN

This man.

The summer expeditions planned along with my very sporting and physically strong wife were ranging now from the Appalachians out to the Montana Rockies. The trips forged a renewed friendship with a former next-door neighbor who had moved to California.

While on a business trip to Vandenberg Air Force Base, we visited him and hatched a plan to climb Mount Rainier in Washington in August of the following year.

We made our reservations and learned we must attend a snow and ice-climbing seminar the day before and demonstrate our knowledge of ice axe usage, self-arrest, roping up, etc. For many months prior to that summer, I poured over textbooks on mountaineering and visualized, and visualized, over and over, what I knew I would have to show. I scoured catalogs of outdoor gear and soon had assembled the requisite array. I had my wife make me a set of nylon mittens because one author suggested that wool knit finger gloves were OK but that thirty-six knot winds would still chill your fingers. We learned that our seminar would be taught by Lou Whittaker. Lou's brother was Jim Whittaker, the first American to climb Mt. Everest.

By August of 1977, my fifty-one year old body felt like it was thirty-five. I had jogged and exercised until I was a hardened mass of muscle and energy.

I met my friend John in San Jose and we started the drive up to Washington. On the way we passed Mt. Shasta and its stark stature and height on the distant horizon gave me a twinge of doubt about the idea of ascending this type of mountain.

We began to see Mt. Rainier in the distance and its mass alone was so imposing, I began to feel real fear. I tried to be casual and unimpressed to John but my head said otherwise. When I stepped out of the car at the National Park's Paradise settlement outside the guides building, I was looking into the side of that awesome massif. I slowly followed the landscape upward until I was looking straight up at the summit, which was in the clouds. I knew then that I had to find a way out of this. I cannot do this, I was sure.

We had dinner, checked our gear and went to bed early, knowing we had in the next morning a day on the icy slopes in training with the guides. I tossed and turned as the night wore on, thinking of ways to hurt myself during the glacier training so I would be disqualified.

We gathered at the guides building and got our crampons and ice axes and climbed to the training slope where there was a long glissade path. Clad in a nylon rainsuit, I was warned by our guide that such material meant very fast slides.

As we were lined up to demonstrate I recalled all the visualizing I had done and as my turn came, I aced the demonstrations to the instructors. I was supposed to be faking trouble and here I was excelling.

My performance that day assured I was in the real climb teams.

Setting out for the camp at 10,000 feet, I muttered to myself continually over and over "I can't do this, I can't."

Camp Muir was the site of our overnight camp. The weather was cold and the glaciers were firm. We ate and then slept in huts on board bunks. We were awakened at 3 AM to start with lamps out onto the glacier for the summit climb to 14,410 ft. The early departure was necessary because the guides had reports that the glaciers may melt more by noon and that we had to get up and back down to the snowfields earlier in the day.

So we were soon roped up and trudging up a forty-five degree slope, driving our crampon clad boots into the snow, one foot after the other, At a stop in a flat area next to a huge ice cliff the wind was fiercely blowing and my fingers were beginning to freeze.

"Oh, god," I thought, *"don't get frostbitten."*

I remembered the nylon mitts my wife had made. My hands were cold because the wind was forcing its way through the wool mitten weave. Our guide helped me get my nylon mitts on and within a few minutes my hands warmed up, the driving wind now cutoff from piercing through the wool.

We then continued up the slope, occasionally looking down at the dawn and the top of the clouds below us.

One foot after the other, freezing air on my face and sweat on my body, what a combination. This was the hardest thing I had ever done, will we ever get up there I cursed.

Then, suddenly, we were greeted with "You made it. Welcome to the summit of Mt. Rainier. Here, have a bottle of Mt. Rainier beer."

I had done it. I vowed at that moment never to say again the words "I can't do this" about life's challenges. At that moment, a tear rolled down my cheek, then I let out a loud hoot.

Exhausted and dry mouthed, I nevertheless refused the unappealing beer. We all walked around on the edge of the dormant volcano's rim and drank in the horizons and the site of lesser peaks well below us. Photos were in order. Then it was time to start down.

The descent of our team was slowed by the rope-handling of the man in front of me. I was the tail man on the rope. I kept warning him to leave some slack but he couldn't seem to get it together.

Suddenly, he was down and that pulled down our rope team and we all began to shout the required "Falling!" I put my axe into position and slid down the slope wondering if I was about to die in an avalanche or fall into a crevasse, then the team's slide stopped.

The guide checked us out and we continued our descent. That descent was into a cloud layer. The result was a dreaded whiteout. The time dragged as we plodded along the invisible path, finally emerging into a view of a great snowfield sloping below us. Our guide suggested we glissade and so we all had fun sliding swiftly down the mountain on our backs and rumps. The sights of Paradise began to show and we soon were in the warm confines of the guides building turning in our gear.

As dusk approached we said goodbye to our guides, first obtaining a certificate declaring our ascent of the mountain.

Needless to say, John and I were high-fiving with others in our party as we left the scene. We felt very flushed with masculine vigor.

We drove to a restaurant outside of the national park and indulged in a steak and much liquid. We collapsed in the adjacent motel and slept like babies.

The next morning we motored back through the forests of Washington and Oregon as Mt. Rainier slowly disappeared in our mirrors. As we began to see Mt. Shasta to the east, John tossed the idea of climbing it.

"Are you nuts?" I said, "I'm still coughing from mild edema and you want to climb Mt. Shasta." His pleading challenged me and we set into plans for our second fourteener in three days.

Shasta was a mixture of geology. It was glaciated but also had great fields of scree, talus, and boulders. What was noticeable was it was desolate. No one was around. The feeling of fear mixed with our conquest of Rainier was soon won by our machismo, and we bunked into a motel and set up our gear for the morning.

We had to check in with the U.S. Forest Service and then we headed up the mountain. The footing was loose and we steadily gained altitude. About halfway up the mountain we were passed by a young couple with a small child in a backpack. We were impressed by their speed of ascent. We saw them later when they passed us on their way down before we had reached the summit.

We took time to stop at the mud pots (volcanic fissures) and warm our hands as famous John Muir had done decades before.

About two hundred feet from the summit John and I sat down. I was totally exhausted. John left me and skittered up to the summit. I sat, pondered my stupidity in not pressure-breathing as I had been taught to do, and took to pumping my lungs.

With a burst of energy, I achieved the top.

Weirdly, there sat a woman, playing a strange tune on a flute with a hippy flag snapping in the wind.

Time was flying by so John and I quickly turned to start back down. He slowly got ahead of me until we were separated from sight of each other. Darkness began to fall as I approached the spot where John had parked his car, but there was no car and no John.

I decided I was in no danger, that I was at the correct place and that I would curl up for the night, having warm clothing and some snacks in my pack. After I had some sleep, I heard a car coming. It was John. He had arrived at the car well ahead of me, figured I was lost and went driving along the road looking for me.

Once we were together, we went into Shasta City and found a beer and pizza place and proceeded to high-five with some other climbers, finally falling into bed exhausted.

The next day I was winging back to Florida, aching but fulfilled.

Florida Sportsman magazine had also nurtured in me an interest in scuba diving and I enrolled in an NASDS school in Titusville, Florida and got certified. That certification began a series of trips to Florida caves and rivers, and to the Florida Keys, and then to the Cayman Islands.

One day on a flight to Los Angeles from Florida, I sat reading the latest issue of Skin Diver magazine. The guy next to me, bearded and big, noticed me reading it and asked, "Interested in scuba, huh?" That signaled me to start spewing my many adventures as though I were a highly active diver. Later in the conversation, I learned that this guy was an early figure in scuba history, and publisher of Skin Diver magazine.

I wondered if I had exaggerated foolishly to such an audience.

Our first trip to the Cayman Islands was with a friend, and his wife. He had been a test conductor on the Mercury space program. We had a one hour flight on Cayman Airways from Miami. When we landed we found a simple wooden terminal, checked in through immigration in a minute, and then got a cab down the road to an old hotel to register. It was from a bygone era on Grand Cayman. There were two or three high-end hotels along Seven Mile Beach nearer to Georgetown but this place had ambiance, and had a dive shop across the street run by a scotsman. It was American Plan lodging so we had other guests at our table for dinner. One man was a German geophysicist on his way back from South America, another a British city planner on a trip back from South Africa, and so it went, a very cosmopolitan array of people. As to the women among the guests, our wives were the most radiant and glamorous, thus adding to the ambiance felt by us men.

The four of us were amazed at the visibility of the water. My wife snorkeled above us while we three dove from iron shore at the water's edge right into ten feet of water. We wound our way through coral reefs and among sea fans and elkhorn coral statutes.

About 300 yards out was the drop-off. The Caymans are seamounts and the earth surface drops off quickly from the summit above the water's surface.

When you go over the edge to the vertical you see your bubbles change from flowing up perpendicular to the bottom to traveling parallel to what you think is the bottom, a very disturbing feeling. I got a bit nauseous and elected to ascend, besides, we were one hundred feet down and were about out of time allowed there by the diving tables.

The four of us enjoyed romantic dinner evenings and during the day, when not diving, explored the outer reaches of the island. One stop was at Rum Cove, a thatched hut grill and bar at the end of a long road at the other end of the island. After a delightful lunch with a tropical drink, we explored other isolated coves and beaches.

Moonlight on the water prompted us to try a night dive. We were amazed at how brilliant and colorful the coral looked when illuminated in our flashlight beams.

The end of our stay came all too quickly and we were soon winging home on a shiny jet airliner, with Caribbean music in our headsets, and a cocktail on our tray. Even the ending of our trip had an ambiance that only can be described as a dream come true.

The following summer we did the same trip again, this time joined by one of our fellow engineers and his wife. That tripled the fun, the laughs, and the mood.

CHAPTER 15

INTEGRATE, TRANSFER & LAUNCH (ITL)

In the late 1970's the post–Apollo era had produced a new concept, the Space Shuttle. Our USAF people were directed to cooperate and co-mingle with Kennedy Space Center design and operations personnel. I was given the management responsibility of an office for our company at KSC.

Meanwhile, USAF spacecraft planners were becoming interested in the shuttle and the order came to us to monitor and influence the Shuttle launch facility designs. We began compilation of a facility requirements document for all known USAF spacecraft programs.

The facility designers at KSC had spent considerable effort trying to collect requirements from the NASA spacecraft programs, but with lesser success. Having to move forward and realizing that most of the requirements were generic and that we had a document ready, they adopted our concepts and requirements for pad spacecraft usage.

Later, when the NASA centers got their needs collected, they were asked to look over the USAF input. They heartily endorsed the data.

In later years, it was a good feeling to see our ideas embodied in those towering structures.

The presence of the Space Shuttle and its facilities was an every day experience for the local space community. Evident to everyone was the vehicle flow from the giant Vertical Assembly Building where the orbiter was integrated to its solid rocket boosters, and fuel tank, then via the monstrous crawler to the launch pad. That flow was a repeat of the method used by the Apollo moon program: Integration of stages in shelter, roll to the launch pad, run readiness checks, and launch.

That integrate, transfer and launch (ITL) flow was also envisioned by the designers of the Titan facilities, but was not used as designed, sad to say. There was not enough USAF budget money to equip the upper levels of the Vertical Integration Building with payload facilities, so, after a Titan vehicle was stacked and checked out, it went to the launch pad to serve as a support stand for spacecraft payloads.

That flow was called factory-to-pad. The method wasted time and resources. This concept was used for many years until faster launch rates were sought. I spent many years of my career trying to get programs to complete the integration off pad, but retired still striving for it. As time went on the method we sought was implemented.

The election of Jimmy Carter as President resulted in a decision to move USAF spacecraft programs to the Shuttle. Most of our team was not thrilled with the decision because it was a tremendous jolt to planning and designs.

We did sigh with relief that most of the spacecraft facilities were ready for such a decision.

And so, the Shuttle payload launch planning activities began.

One of our major programs was among the first USAF payloads to fly on the Shuttle with Gary Payton as payload specialist. He had been at the Cape years before as a young officer and I had spent many hours with him giving him benefit of my experience in launch operations.

The launch was a great success. I had asked Payton to visit our staff after the flight, and show his films and award our staff some mission pins I had procured. For the music background of his flight video he chose "The Way We Were" and his presentation had our female staff members in tears as the earth moved past the orbiter windows.

After the staff event, I took him to lunch at the Cocoa Beach Pier where we were seated at a window table that was exactly over the line of breaking waves below. As we chatted about the flight and other memories, I noticed he was looking a little pale, and then he clutched the table.

I asked, "Are you OK?"

"Sorry, Ernie, I guess the motion of the waves below us gave me a little vertigo."

I thought to myself, an astronaut with vertigo from wave action?

"OK," I said, as he got his bearings, "Tell me, how many of you guys get sick in orbit?'

"Most all of us do experience some, but medications from the flight surgeons pretty much solve that," he explained.

As we left the pier I thanked him and bid him farewell, saying to myself as I had done before, *'there goes a future general'* True to my prediction, he did earn the civilian equivalent to a three star general, and later was appointed as Deputy Undersecretary of the Air Force for Space Programs.

One historical note little known about Payton is that he is one of only two USAF astronauts to have gone into orbit as of this writing, all others being NASA assignees. The other was Bill Pailes who flew in October, 1985. While visiting the USAF Museum at Wright-Patterson, Ohio, I noticed an astronaut display that did not explain that, and I pointed that out to the very appreciative curator. This unusual designation situation occurred because of the secret status of the spacecraft on Payton's flight.

KSC continued busy with many successful Shuttle launches, including ours, and we all began feeling that our industry had figured out how to do its thing.

Then, one very cold day, January 28, 1986, all eyes at the Cape were fastened on NASA's imminent launch of the Space Shuttle Challenger. Weather was dry and cold, a great day for a static electricity incident, I thought. The solid rocket motor engineers on our staff were walking up and down the halls of our USAF building mumbling that "it's too cold to launch, the o-rings will crack".

Our staff was not participating in the launch so our comments had no established communications channel to report such feelings.

One thing was important to us. Colonel Onizuka was on this flight. He was a close associate of Payton's, both having flown their first flight together almost exactly a year prior to Challenger. The countdown surged on, with little or no commentary regarding the cold. Our staff migrated outside into the clear, freezing Florida air and watched as the count reached zero and the huge vehicle lifted into the sky. Then, as it roared away on its trajectory, the vehicle exploded.

Some of my engineers who had gotten to know Onizuka grieved for several hours.

For weeks after, there was a feeling of corporate guilt throughout the entire space industry. It meant there would be a presidential commission and a thorough review of all of our hubris-driven attitudes and culture.

The loss of Challenger marked, for me, a period of phasing out of active employment that I had arranged with my company. I prepared my successor, and my staff with last thoughts and encouragement.

It was time to retire, and to do something else with my life, time to live my next twenty years.

On August 2nd, 1986, I drove off of the Cape for the last time. I had surrendered my access-laden badge, and I felt powerless, and alone. One final wave to the security guard brought a tear to my eye.

I was now a part of history. That had been my dream, and it was now true.

CHAPTER 16

THE DESCENT OF MAN

This man, and his loving guardian angel, too.

While musing one spring day about travel plans, my wife and I received a letter from John, my Mt. Rainier buddy, inquiring if we would be interested in a week-long backpacking trip into the downstream reaches of the Grand Canyon, and he emphasized this was not just the standard tourist Bright Angel Trail thing.

We eagerly examined the details of his proposed trip, assured we wanted to take part.

The plan was to meet on the North Rim of the immense chasm, and descend via the Bill Hall Trail, down through various strata of the canyon, and then on until we reach Deer Creek, site of a falls at the Colorado River. That description was enough and we began eager planning of a trip out west culminating in meeting John. The canyon event was to be a trip of five men including me, and one woman, my wife. John had assured us that sleeping under the stars or cliff shelter would be OK and advised leaving our tent home.

We had read of the Havasupai tribe existence in Havasu Canyon about sixty miles south of the national park on the Colorado, so we decided to travel there first.

After a routine excursion toward Arizona across the southern states on Interstate 10, we accessed the famed Route 66. It took us to a lonely road that led fifty miles north to a parking area. It was the head of an eight mile trail down to Havasu Canyon. The tribe had a lodge there near the famed falls on a tributary to the Colorado.

Along that fifty-mile long access road we had passed tribes people picking nuts from the pinyon pines and great strata of varicolored rock made orange by the afternoon sunlight. When we arrived at the lot we found a paved area with several cars. We set up our van camper for the night and went to bed.

We awoke to the sound of someone pounding on the van body.

"Can you help us?" asked a feminine voice.

"We have car trouble and need to get a message to Los Angeles, I see you have radio equipment. Can you call LA?"

I responded to the affirmative and invited the woman into the van. She gave us a phone number in an LA suburb and I fired up my amateur radio transmitter, tuned to forty meters, and called CQ, Anaheim. Frankly, I expected no answer but unbelievably, a station called from Anaheim, and only a few streets from her business location. Her message was an important one and it went right out and a confirmation was received back to us. She considered our action routine. I considered it miraculous. The next morning, very early, the Arizona State Police arrived and got her help. A few months later we received a wonderful gift from her.

By 8 AM we were ready to begin our trek down into the canyon. Our first experience other than the gorgeous canyon walls was the sighting of beer cans littering the trail. After about an hour's hike, we found out why. A mule train loaded with supplies for the lodge, led by a Havasupai brave drinking from a beer can, passed us. Before he went out of sight ahead, we saw him toss a can aside.

Finally, after four hours of hiking through wonderful views, but dodging beer cans, we sighted the lodge ahead and were soon checking in at the adobe building. The lodge, and our room, turned out to be quite nice and we rested. We awoke and headed for the cafeteria where guests and resident tribes people were eating. Then we took a walk to the awesome Havasupai Falls. We watched tribal entertainment that night and then early in the morning headed back up the trail.

We found the van safe and sound and drove that day to meet John at the North Rim of Grand Canyon National Park.

We found everyone gathering at the parking area and got our gear in order, filling our water containers with that most precious of all things in the desert.

Very soon, we were going over a cliff and down a near vertical slope. What a way to start the adventure. My wife's knees were just not strong enough for the vertical load and we removed her pack and handed it down the cliff face until we found the beginnings of a less violent trail slope where she could manage it again.

The canyon environment was in the seventy degrees temperature zone and it was a gorgeous day, but it was the end of September, and snow at the canyon could occur, especially off the North Rim, which is higher than the South Rim, and is high desert climate.

Our trip was set for seven days (six nights) of backpacking into true wilderness. John had mapped out the water stops and we had no problem with that. After great nights in perfect camps, we finally were nearing the Colorado River on a descending trail. The weather was hot.

Suddenly, coming around a bend in the trail from behind a huge rock walked a gorgeous blond in a bikini. The males in our group, who hadn't seen a woman other than my wife for three days, were delirious and began fawning over this creature.

"Where did you come from? Where are you going?" asked one panting member of our group.

The blonde replied, "Oh, I'm with a raft trip group on the river. I decided to hike the next leg of the trip from Deer Creek to the next landing." John added that this was common. After a few more minutes of embarrassing gawking by our friends, we headed down for Deer Creek.

Our campsite at the river was perfect and we had a wonderful and romantic time in the water and sleeping in the cliff slots. John showed us where we were on the map, and indeed, we were a long way from anybody.

On the second day of heading up and out of the canyon, we were carefully watching for each stone cairn that marked the trail, and the distance between members of our group was stretching out. When sunset came and we made camp in some fine rock overhangs, we realized that one member of our group had not come into camp. We nervously waited for a couple of hours and still no hiker arrived. We decided to bed down and wait until morning to see what the situation was to be by then. The missing hiker was experienced and we knew that if lost he would stop and wait for daylight. It was a moonlit night so he had some advantage out there alone.

Fortunately, he sauntered into camp about midnight. He knew after an hour or so of not finding us that he had made a wrong turn at a trail cairn. We all went to sleep, soundly.

As we trekked up and out of the canyon, we could see that it was snowing up at the top, but was still about sixty-five degrees where we were. We got to the top that afternoon and our cars, and the roads, were indeed covered with snow.

We all said our goodbyes and my wife and I headed south as fast as we could, and on home to Florida. A wonderful, and remote, adventure we will never forget.

CHAPTER 17

FORTY-NINE OUT OF FIFTY

By 1986 I had attended school for twenty years to prepare to work, I had worked for forty, and now was determined to play for twenty more.

Our daughter had graduated from the University of Miami and had married. Our son had his degree in Engineering Technology from the University of South Florida and was married and working at the Kennedy Space Center.

Any ideas of relaxing after my retirement date were dashed quickly. I was elected President of the Florida Trail Association in 1987, and took on the task of rebuilding it after finances were found inadequate to support its needs. That effort required almost a year and a half of three-hour weekly trips to and from its offices in Gainesville in order to stabilize the organization. I quickly learned that running a non-profit corporation with a large volunteer constituency was no easy task.

Determined to make the most of my retirement years, my wife and I began intense use of time for recreation. By summer 1988 the FTA problems had been mitigated and we planned a trip to climb Mt. Whitney, the tallest peak in the lower forty-eight states. We invited

Charlie Monson, a retired USAF officer, to join us. His idea was to have us drive to California, enjoying the time and tourism on the way out, while he hitched a USAF flight to a California airbase to arrive about the time we'd arrive there.

So Jean and I worked up a route that took us through several of the national parks of the Grand Staircase in Utah and Arizona. Our trip included Mesa Verde, Canyonlands, and Arches. As we neared California I began a series of phone calls to Charlie to see where we would pick him up. Each time, he would postpone telling us. I remember pleading with him from a phone booth at a desert gas station to tell us which air base. The tumbleweed was blowing against the booth and the wind was filling my mouth with grit as I shouted into the handset. Finally he confirmed Nellis Air Force Base as the place.

The pick up event went OK and we drove to Lone Pine, California, and picked up provisions and then proceeded across the Owens Valley desert toward the Whitney Portal campground. That drive went through Alabama Hills, a famous Hollywood filming location for desert backgrounds.

After a night's rest, we started for the boulder field at 12,000 feet. The scenery along the lower part of this hike was filled with waterfalls, mountain views, and forests.

The three of us were all in our sixties, and the younger people along the climb were interested in seeing how we old people did. That made me recall the time when my bride was thirty-three and we were hiking up 6600 foot Mt. LeConte in North Carolina to spend the night at the lodge there. Back then my wife complained that she could not breathe, that she couldn't make it to the top, but she did. Now here at age sixty-four she was hiking up Mt. Whitney in California, the highest mountain in the U.S., and cruising right along.

We ascended through the tree line and arrived at the 12,000 feet encampment area. I found the campsite I had used when I climbed Whitney a few years before with my Grand Canyon guru friend,

John. There we pitched our tent for the night. We could see the pass in the peaks that the trail went through onto the west face of Mt. Whitney. We would use that the next day.

Relief of our bowels provided an unusual experience. The U.S. Forest Service had constructed a dry, compost type latrine in this camping area, and when you sat on that one-holer you were looking out from 12,000 feet across one hundred miles of mountains and desert. When the latrine fills up with dried waste, the government removes it by helicopter.

The next morning, after a nourishing breakfast in the clear air, we packed up and started up the last 2500 feet. We went across the snowfields, through the pass and started up the west face. Now the air was getting thinner, and we used our power-breathing technique. It was exhausting, literally. Finally, after trudging slowly along, we all three arrived at the summit. A small group of younger folks applauded as we crested.

Jean found a good rock to sit on and took her trail mix from her pack to celebrate and nourish. She laid her gorp sack down for just an instant when a marmot dashed from a hole and ran off with it.

After high fives with other climbers, we went down the same way we had ascended and made the long all day descent to the campground, getting cheers along the way from the younger crowd.

We unpacked our gear and went into Lone Pine for the evening and a long night's sleep under fresh white sheets. After a great breakfast, we took Charlie to another air base for his flight home to Florida. We then started on a return trip home with interesting visits in Arizona and New Mexico.

During these trips, the number of states we had visited was increasing quickly, and part of our trip planning involved seeing if we could add to the number and reach forty-nine.

In continuation of living our retirement years fully, we kept looking for unusual activities and came across "Hike Inn-to-Inn". A group of seven inns in Vermont had organized a package deal whereby they fed and housed you one evening, then after a superb breakfast drove you, and your own car, to where you wanted to hike to the next day plus packed you a trail lunch. The next inn did the same thing. The most interesting experience about this trip was the ambiance of these outstanding inns, the cuisine, and the past activities of the innkeepers. Among former jobs of these folks were CIA agents, Wall Street brokers, Peace Corp workers, and professorships. My background in the space industry added to the mix.

We loved tropical weather in winter and we loved backpacking but not in winter. So to satisfy both criteria we configured a trip to St. Johns Virgin Islands National Park. Anyone who has travelled to the Caribbean in January knows that three dollars a night is a good deal. That's what the National Park Service was getting for a campsite at Cinnamon Bay on St. Johns.

We drove to Miami then took a flight to St. Thomas and then a ferry to Cruz Bay. I thought we looked odd amongst the travelers because our backpacks mixed with our older age appearance didn't look typical. While waiting for a jeep ride to Cinnamon Bay we met a young man and he started to chat with us. He said he admired our youthful travel method and he asked about our hometown. When queried by us likewise, he said he had been a writer in Hollywood, had produced some B films, and had owned a Mercedes, and a fancy pad in Santa Monica. He went on to tell how he was restless, needed new inspiration and that he was on his way around the world for a few years, working as a bartender. Our jeep arrived and we left him without learning his name. We often wonder what became of his life.

We checked in to the Cinnamon Bay campground, pitched our tent ten yards from the beach, and walked up the hill to the cafeteria. For seven days, we beachcombed, snorkeled, and hiked. One day we went over the mountain range and down in to Little Lameshur Bay. It was deserted. Our picnic lunch, wine, and the weather made a perfect mix, romantic as anyone could imagine. Finally, in the afternoon, a ketch sailed in at the opposite end of the beach. A couple came ashore there in a dinghy. Our paradise had been dashed. Anyway, it was time to hike back over the mountain.

After showers, we took our jeep ride into Cruz Bay and went to an open-air thatched roof restaurant on a hill overlooking the bay, and a gorgeous sunset. Jean was silhouetted against the setting red sun. She had never looked so beautiful.

A delicious Caribbean dinner, wine and mints topped off the dining.

We wanted to stay on St. Johns forever but the spell was broken the next day and we traveled home. We had experienced another of our American dreams.

CHAPTER 18

HURRICANE ANDREW

Our daughter and her husband had lived in their tri-level home in a tropical development in Cutler Ridge near Miami for several years and had a family of two by 1992. Their second child was a boy.

Idyllic as it was, the normality was broken when our grandson was diagnosed with Pervasive Development Disorder (PDD), which is listed under the broader name of autism. Their adjustment into a different life was proud, intelligent, and awesome to watch. It was this little but strong family that was to endure the historic ravages of Hurricane Andrew with courage, resolve, and calm heroism.

Having a family in Miami gave me special reason to hover over the Hurricane Andrew position reports coming in on my high frequency radio equipment on Sunday, August 23, 1992. The storm's path was on top of the 25 degrees, 25 minutes parallel of north latitude. Our daughter's neighborhood highway was 216th Street. On a street atlas I found the two were the same line. She was located just a few blocks away on 219th.

We called her and established a scheme to use the telephone answering equipment, which we each had, to have her communicate their welfare after the storm passed. With that we wished them well, and went back to watching the storm progress.

The reports that the storm was gathering intensity were ominous and I alerted my wife that we best begin assembling food, fuel, and supplies to help them stabilize after the storm passes.

I called a friend for a generator to borrow, bought fuel cans, and fuel, and diapers (our grandson was an infant). My wife bought food and household supplies and we stood ready to leave when the all clear was given.

We watched in near horror as the TV displayed the howling winds and rain pelting the southeast tip of Florida. Reports of Category 3 and 4 gave us further cause to tremble at the thought of our little ones in so much danger (our granddaughter was not yet two years old).

The storm slammed into the landfall on Monday morning, August 24th. We called their home mid-day and could not get through after several tries. With that result I decided it was time to roll. We left an announcement on our phone that we were heading their way with supplies and all.

We got on the Florida Turnpike at Fort Pierce. Tolls had been cancelled. We entered a strangely small stream of traffic heading south. We especially noticed out-of-state electric utility trucks in the stream.

As we entered the Fort Lauderdale area, we began to see minor damage from the storm. The damage and debris then began to mount into devastation as we passed the National Hurricane Center. There the radar antenna was destroyed, and the roof stripped clean of antennas and sensors. Hotel walls were blown in, all windows were blown out, and shingles of all types stripped from roofs for as far as you could see. Street signs, interstate signs, stop signs, traffic lights all gone. The scene was one that a forty-mile wide tornado would produce, not a hurricane.

The further into the disaster scene we went, we found that the number of people out and about was minimal, police cars were few, and downed electric lines were still sparking dangerously in the middle of streets.

During our arrival phase, I had been monitoring the VHF radio band of the public safety services, and of the amateur radio stations.

What I heard was an eerily silent radio spectrum. I realized the antennas of virtually every service had been blown away and crashed to the ground.

We came to 219th St. and headed toward the entrance to our family's subdivision, dodging the hanging traffic lights, downed signs and utility poles. The fronds of the royal palms on the boulevard were stripped clean, producing a weird scene. As we drove into the area, houses were flattened, water pipes were sticking out from ruined structures in ghastly, awkward positions.

As we got further into the area we noticed a transition of damage from completely flattened to one of erect structures with smashed out windows and missing roofs. We found out later that this was because the builder had changed from frame construction to concrete block and stucco.

My wife and I were sobbing uncontrollably. I could hardly steer through the nail-laden wood in the roadway until finally we turned onto their street.

Our daughter was standing in front of their erect but severely damaged home. We got out of the car and embraced with her stating quickly that they were all OK. After the tears stopped flowing we all began unloading the supplies and firing up the generator.

Late that Tuesday evening, I was standing in their driveway next to my van, which bristled with antennas for my amateur radio and weather service work. Up walked a man with a .45 caliber sidearm in a shoulder holster. He immediately introduced himself as neighbor and that he was a sergeant at Homestead AFB, which had been demolished by the storm (and abandoned by the Air Force later). He asked me if I had communications and after I affirmed that, he said that we and another sergeant from the base were the security for this area until we could contact any law enforcement.

That morning, I had contacted the South Dade Emergency Operations Center and advised I had comms. They immediately asked me if I was able to contact Tallahassee. I could, and their question enlightened me to the gravity of the communications damage.

We did not see a police car until Wednesday evening and it was a Charleston, South Carolina police cruiser. Their mayor knew the gravity of the problem in Miami, and with the experience of hurricane Hugo had dispatched his force before the storm had barely cleared South Dade.

On that Wednesday evening, the sergeant came running up to me, out of breath, and requested that I advise South Dade EOC that looters were at houses across the lake from my daughter's home. After I dispatched my message to the EOC, the sergeant and I got into a position where we could see across the lake. It was dark and we had no idea which house was endangered. Suddenly, bright lights from the police search beam and headlights illuminated the robbers looting appliances from a house. We watched their arrest and departure with special pride.

I spent the rest of the week sending hours of health and welfare messages from my van, accompanied by my son-in-law who was my local knowledge guy. Even he did often not know where we were. One way homeowners were helping was by spray-painting their address on their garage door. Today we have GPS to mitigate that problem.

On Saturday, I was dispatched to extreme west Dade County and had to cross US1 on the way. It was bumper-to-bumper as far as you could see. I sat perplexed at an intersection unable to cross when I realized I had a flashing yellow light and official comm signage. After I switched on my light, a National Guard traffic controller stopped all lanes of US 1 traffic and ushered me across.

My duty continued in Miami while my wife took the grandkids home to Cocoa Beach, with the help of our son and daughter-in-law.

Memories of that week, and TV footage of Andrew, always choke me up. I vowed I would be ready for any storm to follow, and that we radio amateurs in Brevard County, would respond with still more capable mobile comm facilities.

Andrew had been a nightmare, plain and simple.

CHAPTER 19

CANCER!

Now sixty-five years old, drawing Social Security, and eligible for Medicare, I wondered how many years I had left in my American dream. My father had died of cigarette-induced cancer but Mom was still alive. Her sisters were all into ages of longevity. I felt my chances were pretty good.

One day in the months after Hurricane Andrew, after a night of unexplainable weakness, a trip to the bathroom to void resulted in the shocking presence of dark, red blood.

I went immediately to our nearby clinic. By the time the doctor examined me the amount of blood was decreasing. She ordered tests to check for infection, and scheduled me to see a local urologist. The next day I was in his office early. He made a hematology slide and told me he wanted to do a cystoscopy the next day to look into my bladder. When he looked into his microscope he confirmed abnormal cells were present.

The next morning I was counting the overhead light fixtures as my Gurney was pushed down the hospital corridor to the operating room. I was to undergo a full procedure under full anesthesia.

When I awoke in recovery, my urologist was at my side. Quickly he told me I had bladder tumors and the pathology showed malignancy. He told me he had scheduled me for surgery the following week to remove the growths. He said my lesions were in the early stages and he felt sure he could excise them.

I was, as most people are, shocked by the word cancer. I envisioned a life of urine bags, catheters, and radiation. After the initial impact of the diagnosis was over, I realized it was time for a bit of mountaineering, that is, one step at a time.

The day of surgery came and it went well. My doctor said he had removed all the tumors and, after some chemotherapy, I should be fine. He then scheduled me for office visits. At those visits, the nurse ingested into me a chemical that was then held in the bladder as long as possible, physically sloshed around, and then expelled. This I accomplished with much duress and stinging pain over several visits.

Cystoscopy was used to see the effect of the chemotherapy. After several weeks, my doctor felt that I was not reacting well to the therapy. He said that after the surgery and chemo effects were long gone, he was going to use immunotherapy, with a serum used in Europe, called the bacillus of Calmette and Guerin (BCG).

Time came for that application and I ingested the vaccine via a catheter. After six weeks of six treatments, time was allocated for response. When my next cystoscopy showed a dark, sinister bladder interior, my urologist told me he was perplexed. He said he was referring me to a famous urology oncologist at Gainesville, Florida's famed Shands Hospital. To me, that was a death knell. I envisioned trips for radiation, and felt nothing was working and that I must start getting my affairs in order. I passed the word to friends and began to wind down my participation in outside activities.

Prayer was an important part of my daily regimen by this time.

I thought about how my obituary would read and abhorred the typical phrase "Mr. Baldini died after a long battle with cancer". I always thought it is strange that you never see news reports that read "He won a long battle with cancer". Yet people are doing that every day.

After a very depressing ride to Gainesville, we walked into the urologist's offices with my pathology reports and gave them to the expert.

He left then came back into his office after examining the file, and said, "Mr. Baldini, you are going to be fine."

My jaw literally dropped, and I asked, "I don't understand, my doctor had said things looked so bad."

He answered, "You have results that look bad but are good signs of action by the BCG therapy. Your doctor has just not seen enough of the range of appearances of successful immunotherapy ingestions. He was correct in sending you up here for further analysis." The doctor then advised that he wanted me to heal a while and then he would do a cystoscopy himself to confirm the cancer was gone. This he did after a few weeks and everything looked fine.

Meanwhile, at Cocoa Beach, my local urologist was nervous about possible metastasis in my pelvic area resulting from the original bladder tumors. He performed an ultrasound on my prostate gland, taking a biopsy. During my next visit, he gave me the bad news: I would need surgery to remove prostate tumors. Having been through the bladder problem, I felt some confidence that I would somehow get through this OK.

One of my immediate options was the placement of radiation seeds in and around the tumors. A consulted oncologist felt I was an excellent candidate for a cure so that was my obvious choice. The oncology-urology team surgeons then placed sixty-five pellets around my groin during a full anesthesia procedure.

In all of the many yearly cystoscopies since then there has been no evidence of recurrence. I am a cancer survivor. My father did not survive his cancer. I recall the question my urologist asked me that day when I awoke from my very first cystoscopy: "How many years did you smoke?"

Another nightmare had occurred among my American dreams.

CHAPTER 20

LAST TOURIST TO ALASKA

It was August 1994, I had survived cancer and life had renewed meaning. It was time for Alaska. We made our travel plan: drive the van up, attend the American Hiking Society meeting, and ferry back to Seattle.

We headed up to and across Wisconsin. We rolled through the small farm towns in Minnesota. We were looking for the "North Woods" ambiance but it was hard to sense.

Each night campgrounds were less crowded. We crossed into Manitoba. The countryside was treeless and only silos arose from the fields. Wheat alternated with sunflowers. We stopped for lunch in a small Manitoba town. We experienced good food, great price and an ambiance of which the townsfolk were unaware.

Next, we crossed the golden prairies of Saskatchewan, and in the distance arose the shining spires of downtown Regina, looking almost surrealistic. Soon through it, we camped in a provincial park that commemorated the plains Indians herding of buffalo into the landforms of valleys and bowls so they could be run off the cliffs for slaughter.

We reached Edmonton, Alberta and visited the Edmonton Mall, the largest in the world. Our view was that we were leaving the complete infrastructure, the trappings of full commerce and industry, and stores for everything. In western Alberta, we camped at a provincial park and the ranger told us we were smart to be traveling at this time of year.

Dawson Creek, British Columbia (BC), was next and the beginning of the Alaska Highway. We noted very light north-bound traffic and wondered if we were stupid to be going to Alaska by auto at this time of year.

The highway was a monument to the U.S. Army Engineers and their role in 1942 of laying a road through forests, over bogs and mountains, and on permafrost, to Alaska. The stories of gravel, dust, broken headlights and windshields, and trucks, trucks, trucks, were no longer true. The Canadians had made it into a first class highway.

Ft. Nelson, BC presented self-serve gas stations, modern motels, and salad-bar equipped restaurants, but the ambiance was evident: dusty pickup trucks; booted, bearded truckers; and a dusty, winter-beaten look to the exterior of the buildings. Landscaping in this land of thousand-mile forests was not to be seen.

Finally came the Yukon. The expectation of lumber camps, and dirt streets that our Hollywood-trained minds conjured up, died away as we arrived in Watson Lake. There a neatly uniformed officer of the Royal Canadian Mounted Police appeared at our van window, issuing a speeding warning. We went on to famous Whitehorse, Yukon. It looked like most small American cities do, parking meters and all. We walked to a café that had been reviewed by New Yorker magazine.

Driving on, traffic began to decrease and road condition began to deteriorate. It was narrower with more frost heaves but, thankfully, no chuckholes. We arrived at the junction of the Alaska Highway with the Haines Highway, a road we were to travel on the trip back to the ferry at Haines. Notable about Haines Junction was the presence of the Kluane mountain range, with snow-capped peaks, standing vertically almost in the center of town. We crossed a causeway in Kluane National Park, the mountains rising up out of the water of Kluane Lake. We thrilled at the scenery and the feeling of knowing that to the west lie a hundred miles of ice-field wilderness. The temperature was beginning to lower each night and the daytime was in the high fifties. After a night in a lodge, the next morning found us approaching the last large zone of construction on the Alaskan Highway.

Long stretches of gravelled, temporary roadbed rattled our van as the giant road machines worked feverishly to beat the winter deadline. We reached Beaver Creek, Yukon. It was cold and wet and we were hungry. The Beaver Creek Lodge looked the part, with the ever-present pickup trucks. The bar was populated with big, bearded construction workers. We sat down and guzzled hot coffee and a fine sandwich, interspersed with a conversation with an Indian. His reason for being there was to buy whiskey.

Anticipation of the U. S. border came upon us. We passed Canadian customs and as we crossed the line, we recited our Stars and Stripes Forever ditty. We have done it at every state and national border crossing for many, many years.

The road was terrible. We wondered why the Alaskan and Federal governments would present such a poor greeting to Alaska visitors. Finally it smoothed out as we approached Tok, Alaska.

Tok was wide and flat. We found Moon Lake State Park and the sites were empty except those at the lakeside had floatplanes tied up. We had found a bush pilot's lake. We later learned that one pilot had taken a father-in-law deep into the Wrangell mountain range about ninety minutes flight time away for a mountain sheep hunt and had come back for the son-in-law. As we motored toward Fairbanks, we came first to North Pole, Alaska, so named to lure a toy manufacturer there. We pulled into a mall plaza and parked, debating whether to visit the ATM at the bank to our right or go to the mall to our left. We chose the mall. When we came out and got in the car, we saw a policeman waving people away from the bank. Then I saw another cop with his rifle aimed at the bank. Turning on the scanner, we heard them saying the suspect had been apprehended and the FBI was on their way. That afternoon we arrived in Fairbanks, a modern

American city and made arrangements for an Arctic Circle trip, a riverboat cruise, and a tour to Prince William Sound to see the glaciers on the last day of that tour's season. When we watched TV that night the news told of a bank robber at North Pole and that he had taken hostages!

The riverboat cruise included a visit to an Indian village (which gave employment to the native University of Alaska student guides). At the village, we talked briefly with Mary Shields, a famous dogsled racer, and asked if she knew a friend of ours in Nome. She did, indeed, and the conversation made us feel like old hands in the Arctic.

The next day we went on the Arctic Circle trip along the famous oil pipeline road. Taiga forest slowly gave way to tundra, the pipeline was always near us, and the guide, an accounting student, was very knowledgeable about the pipeline, the geology and the wildlife. At noontime we stopped at the Yukon River for a picnic lunch.

Next, we arrived at the Arctic Circle, 66 degrees north latitude, and took pictures. Here we were, as far from home as we would ever be in our limited travel lifetime.

On the ride back, we stopped at the lodge at the Yukon River to buy our supper. The lodge was one of the remnants from the pipeline construction era and was made of mobile home modules placed in dormitory fashion.

One of the highlights of the trip was now imminent, a visit to Denali National Park, the site of Mt. McKinley, the highest mountain in North America.

As we neared the park, beautiful lodges began to appear. Prominent among them was the Princess Lodge, owned by the famous cruise line.

The next day we drove to the Savage River area to see mountain sheep. Next we donned our daypacks for a hike up Mt. Healy, near the Visitor Center. We left the forest, rose through taiga, and emerged in the tundra above tree line. The next day, frost had fallen and the day was dreary and damp. The tour bus we took was warm and the driver was great. He had come up to Denali every summer for sixteen years from San Diego. His normal pastime is pharmacology.

Our bus came upon a grizzly with two cubs. The mother was digging for a ground squirrel and was oblivious to our presence. Other sightings included caribou, and a very colorful red fox. The driver described the lodges that existed deep out in the park. One, Camp Denali, is a favorite of actor Robert Redford, and he has been known to reserve the entire lodge for himself and his party. The furthest lodge was 80 miles into the park and one was only accessible by plane.

The road was so narrow in places that the drivers had right-of-way rules for passing head-on. The bus reached the Elieson Visitor Center, at the sixty-six mile point. Looking out at the huge park before us with shrouded glimpses of Denali's peak was a once-in-a-lifetime thing.

The next morning was beautiful as we headed south toward Anchorage, stopping to take dramatic pictures of the mountain bathed in the sunshine.

After a camping stop, our expectations of a fishing village, nestled in Alaskan mountains, and plunging into the sea, were fulfilled by Seward. There we stayed in the Marina Motel, within walking distance of everything in town. We got Kenai Fjords Cruise tickets and went to dinner at the local salmon house, topping it off with Chardonnay and a romantic walk along the marina, dripping with ambiance, and my ever-proud Coast Guard cutters.

The next morning we boarded our cruise boat for a day filled with sightings of whales, otters, sea lions, and birds of all kinds, especially puffins. Highlight of that day was a calving glacier.

We left Seward and the drive down through the Kenai Peninsula revealed a modern economy and towns with wide, curbed streets. In Soldotna, we found a restaurant built of hewn and varnished logs, and savored a gourmet lunch.

Our drive headed for Anchor Point, the farthest west point you can drive to on continuous highway in North America and then for Homer, Alaska, and the land spit, where everything is built on pilings. The community is arty and sophisticated. Finishing the day with lunch at a bakery-restaurant we found it was operated by a couple who came to Alaska twenty years before in an old step van, with a sourdough bread recipe their only asset.

We headed back northeast through Kenai, and got on our tour bus for the Prince William Sound tour. As we rode over the Eureka Pass area, I wondered what the weather there would be like on October 3rd when we would be hightailing it southeast for Haines, Alaska to wait for our ferry. We stopped at Eureka Lodge on the summit of the pass for lunch, and stepped out into a freezing wind howling at thirty miles per hour.

We went through Thompson Pass near Valdez, where the snow gets to 700 inches deep in the winter and the highway can only be detected by special poles along the right-of way. We arrived in Valdez in the rain and checked into a hotel then walked to dinner at the Pipeline Club, where, it is said, Capt. Hazelwood and his crew got inebriated the night before the ill-fated infamous Exxon Valdez oil spill. After dinner, we toured the Alaskan Pipeline terminal, which is awesome. Tankers are loaded in thirty-six hours, and oil is stored there only long enough to fill the ships. The next morning we cruised Prince William Sound. We passed Bligh Reef where the Exxon Valdez grounded. Any reasonable navigator, even without modern high-tech radar, sonar and GPS, wouldn't hit that reef without just plain carelessness.

On the cruise we approached Columbia Glacier. Ice was everywhere, some white, some clear, and some deep blue. We watched the helmsman steer the vessel through the ice, simply shoving immense pieces out of the way.

When the ship docked at Whittier, we boarded buses, which were then driven onto Alaska Railroad flatcars. Whittier has no roads into it so the railroad takes the buses through the mountain tunnels to Portage where the buses drive off and return to Anchorage.

Deciding to move our camping, we went to Chugach State Park, an immense park to the east of the city, part of the Chugach mountain range. The peaks were beginning to show snow and temperatures were getting lower.

Next we visited the rapidly receding Portage Glacier south of Anchorage. We stopped along Turnagain Arm (a fjord) to view Beluga whales chasing salmon.

For our need to use a modem we got a motel room, with phone, near the bush pilot airdrome in Anchorage. It was fascinating to watch the small planes take off, wondering where in this great outland they were headed.

Anxious to hike, we went further out into the vast Chugach State Park, up a mountain road to Eklutna Lake. We hiked up a mountain trail to an overlook of a lake nestled amongst tall peaks, and populated only by a lone kayaker, but hiding a bush pilot landing dock at its far end.

When we left the park, the ranger said we were the last campers of the season and as we left, she closed the area and locked the gate behind us.

I spent the next few days at our American Hiking Society conference in Anchorage. It ended and we set out on the three-day trip to Haines, Alaska. We went up over Eureka Pass and then the Alaska Range, where we encountered snow on the highway. It had not yet melted and my wife drove expertly, as I peered down the thousand foot dropoffs at my right-hand.

At Tok, Alaska we ate a big dinner and flopped in bed. When we arose and prepped with a gas fill up, the attendant warned us to be careful. The road to the east was icy and cars had gone off the highway during the night. The next five hours were tiring as we constantly assessed road conditions and drove with tight grip. We came upon one of the vehicles, upside down, about ten feet down the roadbank edge, and next encountered two tractor trailers that had tangled on an icy curve. The road construction between the border and Beaver Creek, Yukon, had progressed but was still incomplete.

There was virtually no traffic as we went into the Kluane mountain range country we had admired on the way up. The campgrounds were all closed, only a lodge or two remained open.

Arriving at Haines Junction, Yukon, we knew we were two-thirds through our worst fear, bad weather. The next morning was clear and the ground covered with frost. Heading down the Haines Highway, which we did not use on the way up, the weather remained cold but dry. The only other vehicle we saw was a Yukon Highway department rig. We were awed by new views of the vast Kluane range, great vistas and ever-rising altitude. We had to go over 9000 foot Chilkat Pass and shivered with anticipation of bad weather. As we entered the high altitude tundra region, a bush plane was landing on a lake to our left. Since there was no one else around, or any structures, we slowed as we passed the lake, to see if the pilot would signal us for help. No one did so, so we went on.

We arrived in Haines and got a campsite. We had missed the ferry to Seattle by a day and now had to suffer through the winter ferry schedule, waiting three days. We also found that Skagway, nearby, had closed for the season. So we filled our days with viewing gatherings of bald eagles.

The ferry arrived and we boarded it for a four-day cruise down the Inland Passage. We had a cozy cabin and enjoyed great food in the dining room. We arrived at Bellingham, Washington and disembarked to great fall weather, and happy to be back in the lower forty-eight.

One of our dreams had been completed and we had done it our way.

CHAPTER 21

NO PLACE LIKE HOME

We set out for home going eastward on US 2 through the Cascades and into the great American desert, stopping at Yakima to see the piles of volcanic ash still evident from the explosion of Mt. St. Helens. Our route then continued across the great northwest, through Idaho to Jackson Hole, Wyoming. We then found US191, America's most beautiful highway. We drove from snow-capped peaks and forests down into Flaming Gorge, through the wonders of eastern Utah, stopped at the Four Corners, and then headed for Florida

As we travelled, I mused about our trip. We had ranged through the geology and weather of the north American continent. Up from the sandhills of Florida, across the Piedmont, over the Appalachians, into the Ohio River valley, crossed a Great Lake, the glacial moraines of Wisconsin, the upper Mississippi. We rolled across the plains and grasslands, over the Canadian Rockies, into the taiga forests of the Yukon, up into the tundra at the Arctic Circle. We sat upon the confluence of the Pacific and Canadian tectonic plates, ever moving and volcanic, sailed amongst the fjords of Alaska and British Columbia, rolled across the great American desert, viewed the endless vistas of the mesas, sensed the sandstone canyons and castles of the Southwest, tasted the dry Texas waters, and the Mississippi delta. We had been hot and humid, cold and humid, hot and dry, and cold and dry. We had driven on ice and snow, in howling wind and rain, and in gorgeous sunshine.

What we had experienced most were the people. Their diversity and what that makes of a nation. The Canadian label on a person means he or she can be of French, German, Ukrainian, Scotch, Irish, Russian, Eskimo, Athabascan, or Tlingit descent. The Alaskans are the same mix but there is, distinctively, an American spirit. The fierce independence of Alaskan thought permeates their society. It is closest to being libertarian, but they don't realize it. The native people there have been given a very fair shake, much more then other native Americans. It is now the proving era for them. Our observations are that they are marginally succeeding, but the scourge of liquor and free money from oil may spoil them.

We found that you cannot really see the land as it was meant to be seen, or to meet the local people in an unhurried way unless it is quiet, the season is over, and you are . . . . the last tourist.

After arriving home and settling into our normal life style, we began to talk about how we were now into our seventies and though still traveling we were slowing down a bit. We reviewed our commitments to the world.

I was serving our congregation as President, spending many hours changing over our church computers, and we were both still working in Florida Trail activities.

The famous real estate boom of this era was in full swing and my wife felt we should consider selling our Cocoa Beach home of 40 years. We realized we were not using the ocean beach three blocks away, had sold the boat and had quit fishing, and also felt more vulnerable to hurricanes. Cocoa Beach was becoming more of a tourist destination than a residential place and the pokey traffic was frustrating. This review got us looking at new places and types of living. After a few years of fun visiting new homes and condos, we found our dream place; a townhouse on the Florida mainland, close to shopping, and one hundred yards from a country club with pool and dining room.

At the crest of the real estate bubble we sold our venerable home on the canal, taking our memories with us to a new life.

CHAPTER 22

SUBDIVISIONS AND COUNTRY CLUBS

We had lived our entire married life in single family homes and we were now, in 1998, moving into a unit in a quadplex building, governed by covenants and by-laws of an active homeowners association (HOA) which was part of a larger master homeowners association.

I remembered my reaction back in the 1960s and 70s when the idea of condominium associations first became popular. That idea had unit ownership of the interior furnishings and the association ownership of walls, etc. I thought at the time that such an arrangement was fraught with complexity and legalistic dilemma. I made sure that our move was into a homeowners association and not a condo, as the other was nicknamed. The associations are governed by officers and boards. I thought then that sooner or later you exhaust the available, qualified supply of people. That, I decided, meant an industry would grow out of need for community managers, paid to run these entities.

Guess what? Today there are thousands of such community managers across the United States, and the legal profession has thousands of lawyers that practice such law, and state constitutions have sections on condo and HOA law.

We moved in and found we had a fine group of neighbors. I was recruited by our HOA to serve as Treasurer. I reluctantly accepted and soon I was briefing our group on the need for reserves for the proverbial rainy day.

Meanwhile, the lure of fine dining just across the road snagged us and we plunked down one thousand dollars to join the country club. I never thought I would be the country club type but I adjusted to the role quickly, addicted to the dessert table at Sunday brunch. We didn't play golf, but did use the pool, especially when the grandkids visited us. What I didn't realize was that we were paying the club for the privilege of buying their food.

History was attached to our unit, we found out. It seems that the club had once owned our unit and used it for housing visiting PGA golfers. Our neighbor told us that Arnold Palmer had stayed in our unit. After learning that, I contacted Palmer's publicist and got a photo, signed by the famous golfer, with a salutation about staying there.

My management skills got me into trouble again when the HOA board asked me to be President after two years as Treasurer. I accepted, reluctantly as usual, and tore into updating the documents, called Covenants, Conditions, and Restrictions (CC&R). I instituted a newsletter to keep everyone informed.

With matters running smoothly in our association, and with competent officers and a professional community manager in place, I began to step back from direct roles, but did advise on financial planning.

The new millennium was imminent and so was our fiftieth wedding anniversary. The club was a wonderful place to hold the celebration and my wife and I invited many friends and relatives to come. It was a grand day, and we had the honor of seeing our old friends again. Many were to pass on all too soon after that.

Age was beginning to show its wear on us and we began to measure out our energy. We were becoming more reflective about life and death, and we kept our advisors busy with trusts, wills, and matters of senior living.

One of our Florida Trail friends organized a "Cross Florida" backpacking trip for seniors over eighty. I was enthused by the idea and joined the planning. It was great to be back on the trail during that week but fate was against me when my back gave out about forty miles into the trip. I knew, down deep inside, that this was to be my last backpack trip.

The idea of "last this, last that" was emerging in talks with my wife. Car, house, dryer, washer, anything we bought was the "last". So the idea of one last hike, without backpacks, solidified. We called it our Golden Hike, ala Golden Pond. It involved hiking in Georgia five miles up to a mountain lodge. We octogenarians made it, much to the surprise of the youngsters who did it that day.

Another manifestation of our age had emerged, we realized. We were celebrating many fiftieth anniversaries of organizations, friends, places, etc. This was especially meaningful in the historical realm of the space industry.

For the 50th anniversary of the Atlas rocket, Lockheed-Martin, now the manufacturer of the Atlas, invited me to attend the final launch of an Atlas-Centaur from Complex 36. I had been in charge of the launch pad's construction and launch conductor of the rocket's first launch. Now it was to all end for that piece of Cape Canaveral real estate.

The launch consoles in the blockhouse contained two sets. The Complex 36A set was now decommissioned, and the 36B set was to be used for the final launch. I arrived at the pad with my copy of the launch countdown for Atlas-Centaur F-1.

Back in 1962, at the first launch, I had the launch team sign it. Now here it was, forty-five years later, sitting in the same place, the launch conductor's console. The present-day crew took many pictures of me, and of the present-day launch conductor next to me.

The countdown progressed ever so smoothly and as it reached zero, and we had liftoff, a tear ran down my face. There were toasts to the event, the company having supplied champagne, and I toasted the crew on behalf of all who had come before.

As we left the blockhouse, and the pad lights were to be turned off for the last time, I stood with the other two guys in the misty dawn, with the LOX vapors wisping across the concrete. It was a scene for a movie. Another tear.

Talk about an American dream.

CHAPTER 23

END OF LIFE IS AN INDUSTRY

This book has chronicled my life story, which has turned out to be an American Dream fulfilled. I wrote it to help others see that they too can reach their dream if they know clearly what that dream is.

But my story, at this writing, isn't over yet.

And there may be nightmares ahead before it is.

In trying to protect our dream through our final days, months, years, whatever, my wife and I have continued to make the choices necessary.

Irresistible force meets immovable object. That comes to mind when I hear people say "Stay healthy so you can live long enough to die in a nursing home". Think about it. We all want to keep on enjoying life, with full health, but there is a limit. No one likes what that limit means.

So, as in all human endeavor, an industry has emerged to help manage that final phase of our lives. The marketplace for senior living dreams has generated some modes. Here I list some of them.

Independent Living—a mode that could be called "condo with a dining room downstairs". What you are independent of is for you to define. Such facilities have lots of staff to make you comfortable, happy and safe, and in some, when your infirmities set in, you can phase right into assisted living.

Assisted Living—this mode has been a great idea of facilities for managing our infirmed years because it provides a place for living and assistance in the daily physical effort of keeping our bodies clean, fed, and medicated. When this assistance changes into nursing is still under debate in the industry, and sometimes when you get too infirmed some assisted living facilities ask you to leave.

Nursing Home—this mode usually means that, in addition to the above, some time during your day a registered nurse will be attending to you, with doctor visits by the facility's physician during a week. This is a more serious, and expensive phase of our aging.

Home Care—this mode means that the services and phases above are brought to you in your own home. It is a growing segment of the industry and can be more economical than the others.

The cost of these choices is the more serious part of keeping our American dreams intact in the last part of our years. The costs may be not only financial but also physical and mental loads upon loved ones who are caregivers or care managers. Whether our society can continue to afford these costs remains an open question.

Let's all hope that our dreams remain intact, that our nation and economy prosper, and that when our time comes, we die in dignity.

Plan ah . . . .

. . . . e

ad

fghjn, mmmmm